Brilliant Business Connections

How powerful networking can transform you and your company's performance

Frances Kay

howto**books**

Published by How To Books Ltd,
3 Newtec Place, Magdalen Road,
Oxford OX4 1RE. United Kingdom.
Tel: (01865) 793806. Fax: (01865) 248780.
email: info@howtobooks.co.uk
http://www.howtobooks.co.uk

British Library Cataloguing in Publication Data
A catalogue record for this book is available from the British Library

Produced for How To Books by Deer Park Productions, Tavistock
Edited by Sarah Cooke
Cover design by Baseline Arts Ltd, Oxford
Typeset by PDQ Typesetting, Newcastle-under-Lyme, Staffs.
Printed and bound in Great Britain by Cromwell Press, Trowbridge,
Wiltshire

NOTE: The material contained in this book is set out in good faith for
general guidance and no liability can be accepted for loss or expense
incurred as a result of relying in particular circumstances on statements
made in the book. The laws and regulations are complex and liable to
change, and readers should check the current position with the relevant
authorities before making personal arrangements.

Contents

Preface

We all know that 'people do business with people'. This is perhaps one of the overriding reasons why most of us would pick the human voice or face to face contact when given the choice over automatic systems and machines. Despite the amazing progress of technology, which enables us to do almost everything instantly and at the press of a button, there is something reassuring and comforting about individual attention and personal service.

Brilliant Business Connections are what everyone who wants to succeed in business really needs. But how do you make them and what should you do to get the most from them? These are the questions I have tried to answer in this book.

For readers who are experienced networkers and have many good contacts, it will inspire you to try new approaches or revise your methods. If you are new to your job or starting out on your career it will help you make the most of the opportunities offered as you meet people in the course of your work.

For many years I have been meeting people and developing professional relationships in the process of my work. People are fascinating, unique and often quite surprising. Many profitable connections and good friendships have resulted and my career and business has become synonymous with connecting people for professional advancement. Referrals, recommendations and business introductions are second nature to me. It is because of the richness of these experiences and the many rewards I have received that I decided to write this book.

There is nothing scientific about the method and the truth is most of us know how to do it! Sometimes however we lack the courage, confidence, time or skill. Many people I know are naturally skilled while others simply require a bit of help and practice.

Whatever your level of expertise, you will find common sense tips, advice and suggestions on how to build your own personal network of connections. Armed with this knowledge you will have greater confidence and progress further and faster with your career and building your business. You will also probably have more fun too! If building pleasant and profitable business relationships is something you would like to do, I hope you enjoy reading this book.

Frances Kay

(1)

Who Needs Business Connections Anyway?

If a man does not make new acquaintance as he advances through life, he will soon find himself left alone. A man, Sir, should keep his friendship in constant repair.

Samuel Johnson (1709–84)

It's not how clever you are, it's not your background, it's not whether you're a man or a woman, it's not your height, it's not your age! It's the power of personal connections that underpins business success today.

A staggering 97% of professionals believe it's who you know, rather than what you know, that's important.

Business today relies more on people skills than on qualifications and experience. No matter how brilliant you are at your job, if you want to get ahead, you need great connections. Working away for hours on end at your desk is no longer enough – get out and get connected!

Task awareness is fine, but being passionate about people will take you further faster.

1

Those who tackle this area and get it right have the opportunity to influence positively the growth and profitability of their business and enhance their career. Achieving goals is far easier with (to quote The Beatles) 'with a little help from my friends'.

DO PEOPLE MEAN BUSINESS?

In a word, Yes! There are two main reasons why you should harness the power of personal connections:

♦ Your company will be more successful. It will stand out ahead of its competitors.

♦ You will progress further and faster along your career path than someone who doesn't.

Making yourself known to the right people is more important now than in the past. Why? Because there aren't so many jobs for life. Workers switch roles and careers far more frequently than they used to. There are an increasing number of entrepreneurs and consultants. For anyone setting up a business and for the self-employed good contacts are essential, particularly when attempting to build or increase your client base.

Personal recommendations speak volumes and are more impressive than the best CV.

If you've tried blowing your own trumpet try asking another person for help. You'll be amazed how much louder it sounds coming from someone else! Today, for all those wishing to reach great heights, brilliant business connections are essential and by far the best way forward.

Developing successful relationships at work needs effort in two ways:

'Business success is 20% strategy, 80% people.' John Sunderland, Chairman: Cadbury Schweppes, addressing HR100 Club – reported in *Management Today*, February 2004.

- ◆ internally, within the organisation or profession
- ◆ externally, among clients, work providers, suppliers.

In both cases, it helps to be confident and have extrovert characteristics. Some people are natural born 'networkers' and have loads of charisma. For others, those skills need to be acquired. It's not difficult if you use some tried and tested methods.

Be flexible!

Remember that the same approach is not right for each contact, much less for each occasion. Finding the appropriate way to further the business relationship-building process is the answer. And this means each day, for each person, meeting by meeting.

So how do you go about making the right connections for yourself and your company?

Building effective relationships in the workplace is the key skill for professional success in the 21st century. It's true that the most successful people and organisations are also the best connected. By developing and nurturing a strong network of personal contacts, you too can be more effective in business and in your career progression.

REASONS WHY IT WORKS

- Managers with great contacts get promoted faster.

- With good relationships in the workplace, you are more likely to be successful when taking charge of new situations.

- Having strong personal networks means higher job satisfaction.

- Problems can be solved faster, before they become crises.

Remember – it's reciprocal. If you help others, they will help you in return.

Is it risky?

Only if you don't do it. You may be a bit apprehensive about moving outside your comfort zone. This sounds far worse than it is. Developing relationships at work is about rapport-building – the intelligent approach to business and career development.

If you're someone who is naturally people-aware, then you probably make connections easily and quickly. Contacts and friends are plentiful and meeting new people is no great ordeal. If you are shy or reticent, don't worry. These skills can be acquired and, with a little practice, they'll become second nature.

TAKE THE PLUNGE

You too can harness a huge amount of power by knowing lots of people. Some of them will be in the right positions to help you or know other people who are. It not only puts you way ahead of the competition – people with good connections are winners, time after time.

James was a whiz with figures. He loved preparing analyses, reports, graphs, charts and diagrams showing the growth rate of the financial products of his company. He had been doing his job for a number of years and was successful, but he knew he was 'stuck' at his present level. He was mid-way up the managerial ladder and wanted promotion so he could achieve his desired career level. Unfortunately James was not naturally gregarious. His brilliance at his job was not helping him in the slightest. His colleagues hardly knew him, had limited appreciation of his work and generally thought he was aloof. When James's director suggested coaching, it unlocked his potential.

It was shyness that was holding him back. James wanted to be able to mix with people, but just felt he wasn't any good at it. The coach encouraged James to pay attention to people who he thought were good mixers and take note of what they did. After a few coaching sessions James announced that he'd 'got it'.

How? He said he'd been standing next to his wife in the supermarket queue as she started a conversation with a complete stranger. He'd realised suddenly that because she was a naturally curious person she talked to people wherever she happened to be. She was always making new friends and coming home with extraordinary bits of information.

If you show curiosity about other people, he said, and make them realise that you're genuinely interested in them, you find people respond positively. James had worked out the *art of rapport-building.*

MAKE THE EFFORT

It's worth it.

At each level in every company or profession, powerful personal connections underpin business success. The formal advantages of good personal connections include:

◆ colleagues work best in co-operative teams

◆ managers get more from their staff through encouragement, motivation and guidance

◆ effective directors provide inspiring leadership

◆ clients enjoy working with you and are happy to recommend you.

And on an informal note, isn't life just easier and more fun when you enjoy good relationships with other people?

Not long ago, I was due to attend a meeting for which I had no enthusiasm whatsoever. It was a hot summer evening in London and I was tired after a day at work. When I arrived at the venue it got worse. The air conditioning in the conference suite was broken – it was stifling. Everyone was hot and flustered. I nearly walked out.

However, as I was already there I decided to stay. I took the first seat available, and struck up a conversation with the person sitting next to me. It turned out to be someone I hadn't seen in 35 years! We'd grown up together during our school days. The result? A friendship rekindled and the bonus of a great new working relationship. This chance meeting and business opportunity could so easily have been missed if I'd not taken that particular seat.

Whether yours is a profession or trade, a commercial or charitable organisation, profit making or not, in the service industry or manufacturing, you will be more successful if you build better relationships with all those who have an impact on your business.

People do business with people they like, trust and respect. Powerful business connections don't necessarily come from people in high places. A small piece of information can make a huge amount of difference. You may often get help from the most unlikely sources. Never forget the power of 'thank you'.

> **TIP**
>
> Brilliant business connections take time. Remember, it's people, not skills, education, qualifications or experience.

Resounding referrals

Not long ago a client wrote a referral letter for me. He described me as being 'unique in establishing and developing corporate networks and relationships. In changing times maintaining networks in physical and personal terms is of paramount importance. Frances's ability to take on this role in an intelligent manner is impressive, representing organisations or individuals, picking up and nurturing the threads of strategic business continuity.'

Impressive? I thought so. I hadn't expected such a great unsolicited testimonial. Do you ever ask people what they think about you? What qualities and attributes best describe you? Maybe a little 360 degree feedback would help. You may be agreeably surprised!

In my work I spend a lot of time persuading people to become less task-aware and more people-oriented. I'm convinced if you can fine-tune the art of rapport-building, it helps strengthen careers and promote business. Not only do I try to match people, organisations and opportunities, I also coach, mentor and train people on the importance of relationship building via their own personal network.

I stress the words 'own personal network' because everyone has one. Some people simply don't believe that. Whether you realise it, pay attention to it, work on it and use it to advantage, everyone has a network. It is unique, like you. It contains a wealth of individuals, information and opportunity. What I hope you will learn from this book is how to put these contacts to good effect.

There is nothing you can't achieve, if you set your mind to it. If you add the power of personal connections to your own individual skills, you will enjoy better, innovative and more profitable relationships with existing and new customers, suppliers, staff, colleagues and superiors. This will help you progress faster.

SMALL TALK MEANS BIG BUSINESS

The reason I agreed to write this book is because I know how much people have influenced my life and the choices I've made. I want to share with you what can be achieved from great external contacts and strong internal relationships. I can prove it's the power of personal relationships and brilliant business connections that really matter.

The Value of Excellent Personal Contacts

Anything worth doing is worth doing to excess.
Edwin Land

So, people do business with other people. If those who you want to be remembered by recollect you favourably the next time you meet, the possible rewards are endless.

Building relationships requires time, commitment and effort. You need to be focused, self-disciplined and have patience. When people like you, they will probably want to do business with you, it's as simple as that. It's all about persuasion and has nothing to do with selling.

R FOR RELATIONSHIPS

Let's look at some R words.

Relationships. Why build them? Two reasons: because it's practical and profitable. The most successful people are the best connected.

Recognition. Creating impact is essential when you meet people. Never underestimate the power of first impressions.

Recall. If someone can recall you easily, you've (hopefully) made a favourable impression when you were first introduced.

Reaction. One of the things you are hoping for is a positive reaction when you encounter someone again.

Respect. Aim to gain their trust. The ability to co-operate with and assist others is vital. You will then earn respect. Don't forget to show it to others in return.

Responsibility. You should take responsibility for your business relationships. That will keep you in control of your personal network. It's worth a lot to you – don't let others mess it up.

Your own network

Everyone has their own group of personal contacts – their unique network. How many people are in yours? Do you value it? How do you use it?

Some ways it can be used include:

- as a **research aid**, for information gathering
- as a **link to new clients** or markets
- to **advance your career** by seeking influential people.

Whatever its purpose, it's a powerful resource.

HOW TO START

The way to build brilliant business connections is a three-part process:

- First, you **network** to make connections.

- Second, you use the **connections** to build relationships.

- Third, your **relationships** used wisely, bring rewards.

A LIST OF POSITIVES

List of positives which can be achieved:

- When you harness the power of personal connections, you will appear to advantage within, as well as outside, your organisation.

- You can chart the success of your own goals and objectives.

- One of the many bonuses is meeting like-minded people.

- Most people have a network of around 250 contacts – and within that there are perhaps 25 individuals whom they know really well.

- You can develop the network you most want, and identify those with whom you wish to build rapport. It is infinitely flexible and adaptable. Your objectives may alter as you go along, but you can change the links and paths to achieve your plans. You can focus on success in both business and career development.

TIP

Put people first – they are the most important ingredient of all. Business effectiveness increasingly depends on interpersonal skills and creating trust is paramount.

SUCCESS = MEASURABLE RESULTS

There are two important things to remember:

- **Internal relationships**. The purpose of building good relationships within your company is to be well informed. This saves valuable time and increases productivity. You also pick up on internal politics and are able to maximise opportunities that come your way.

- **External relationships**. Externally, you will have valuable contacts who act as referrers, bridges, sources, links and influencers to help you achieve your personal goals.

KEY POINT

The key skills required, if you don't already have them, are enquiring, listening, researching and organising.

SOME WINNING EXAMPLES

Here are some case studies of companies that invested time and effort in building the right connections.

Brilliant business introductions
A newly formed IT-based company wanted to find potential investors. They worked hard to develop a network of business connections to help them source potential funds. They spent six months researching suitable prospects, influencers and connectors, to identify a number of venture capitalists and investors. From a number of introductions they found three venture capitalists who were prepared to help them. They now have sufficient investment for their growth over the next five years. Their business is on track to perform to its maximum potential.

Strong strategic alliances
An international firm of consulting engineers wanted to improve their ability to win more business in the UK and Europe. Their business development strategy was drawn up to increase their links with, and standing among, the most relevant movers and shakers in the construction and property industry. By working hard to raise their profile within their profession, they nurtured influencers and recommenders who helped them build strong strategic alliances. They have recently won a number of important construction awards and several internationally acclaimed projects.

Close client relationships
A high-profile practice of UK architects carried out a client satisfaction survey to benchmark their reputation. They compiled questionnaires,

interviewed a selection of clients, prospects and influencers. The results reflected the company's strengths and identified areas where improvement was necessary. By following up on some of the encouraging comments received, the directors were able to acquire repeat business and extension work which increased their annual turnover by almost 20%.

Terrific team building
A charity had to organise a high-profile fundraiser at a time when there were a number of other, similar events. Apathy had set in, take up on tables was slow and ticket sales were sluggish. The organisers needed to harness energy and enthuse staff to take the project forward. By calling in favours from some of the charity's high-profile patrons and supporters, it was possible to rekindle enthusiasm and energise volunteers.

A brainstorming session took place among a group of individuals who had diverse skills and personality types. A number of new initiatives were suggested. Everyone took on a role that most suited their personal strengths. The result: the project went forward with eagerness because volunteers worked harmoniously and productively together and the event was a sell-out.

Smooth succession planning
A global financial institution needed to help some of their executives who were on track for career progression. Although successful within the organisation, a number of these individuals had been appraised as being highly task-aware. Due to their lack of awareness of the importance of personal contacts within the company and weak interpersonal skills, their promotion prospects were on hold.

The company looked within itself and, through its internal network, identified several key individuals who were asked to become mentors for these young managers. By setting up a mentoring and coaching programme, the company was able to help them back on track. Their interpersonal skills increased, they became less task-aware and in addition the company gained the advantage of smoothing their succession planning.

RAPPORT

Here is a mnemonic to help build business connections.

R Relationships
A Are
P Powerful
P Providing
O Opportunities and
R Rewards
T Today

Rapport-building requires the development of a genuine interest in other people. This gives you great advantages over those who don't nurture professional relationships. It involves getting to know people and introducing them to others.

Quality v quantity

If you look at the whole process of developing brilliant business connections, it is rather like a treasure hunt. You never know who you will meet or what you may find out. It can produce the most amazing results.

For years I've been focusing on people rather than tasks, and I've had a number of extraordinary coincidences, lucky breaks and phenomenally successful connections. Some of these are used later to illustrate what can happen when you least expect it.

> You should always try to seek out opportunities for sharing information and contacts wherever you are.

You may need to adopt new habits and move outside your comfort zone from time to time. Remember, when you ask for help from people, always offer assistance in return. Saying 'thank you' costs nothing and gains you so much.

3

The Three-Stage Plan: Step One – Networking

'Smile – it either makes others feel good or makes them wonder what you're up to.'

Found on the Internet

So you're taking action to harness the power of personal connections. It will enhance your career prospects and progress your company's business development. Your goal is to make quality contacts and devise a plan for strategic relationship building. The process starts here.

I am not a networking guru. I don't intend to take up much of your time giving advice on how to work the room and collect business cards. You may wish to try, or have already practised, speed networking – a new and popular way of connecting for business. I expect you are probably familiar with the networking process.

There are many businesses, professional associations and other organisations which offer these forums – whether breakfasts, lunches, or evening receptions. It is a great way to meet people for business development purposes. What happens **after** that initial meeting is what this book is about.

You can't do big business until you've done the small talk

One of the main reasons people network is to create new business opportunities. It's a bit like dating – so you'll need some chat-up lines. When you want to build a relationship, make sure you ask the right questions. It's far more important to be interested, than interesting.

Why networking is essential

Whether you are a self-employed professional or ambitious to succeed in your company, industry or sector, the 'need to know' and 'need to be known by' is an essential business skill.

Networks matter – it's as simple as that. They are part of the corporate survival strategy and a staggering 97% of self-employed professionals rely on contacts and referrals to get work.

Networks enable you to access work, resources and opportunities. They also create a sense of community and rapport and allow you to share experiences with like-minded people.

If you want to assemble or improve your own network, you need to review your existing contacts to see if they are effective and current. Consider the following questions:

- Do you communicate regularly with your own network?

- Do you proactively seek to increase and refresh your contacts?

- Is it a formal or informal arrangement?

- Have you asked your contacts for help or offered support and advice to them?

- Do you keep your network in good shape for easy access and management?

Networks work best with 'give and take'. You only get out what you are prepared to put in. The best networks are information-rich, collaborative, high-trust environments. To be part of a vibrant network it is best to start simply.

Some of the best ways are:

- personal contacts, friends and associates
- ex-colleagues and present co-workers
- alumni networks
- clients and professional contacts
- professional associations
- national umbrella organisations.

These should be a rich source of opportunities. Most successful networks work on the basis of personal introductions and referrals.

The networking process and how it works is probably familiar to you. But for those who want to refresh their networking skills, or have one or two confidence issues, the following key pointers can be used as an *aide memoire* before moving on to the next stage.

GET ORGANISED

Preparation is essential. Proactive business relationships don't happen just by chance. First and foremost have a plan. This really matters. If you don't know why you're doing something, you won't do it well.

If you're a bit reluctant to move out of your comfort zone, preparation helps. The more industry functions and business events you attend, the less threatening they will be. To have a vibrant network you need to keep widening your range of contacts. This is the purpose of networking – to get out more!

- When you attend an event, ask yourself beforehand, how important is it? Your **time is valuable** – always make the best use of it you can. Should you be accompanied by a colleague or do you go alone? Is one person sufficient? Would two be overkill?
- **Study the delegate list** beforehand, if possible. This way you maximise the opportunity to reach the right people.
- Ensure that you are appropriately dressed. Always **check the dress code** – appearances can make or break an encounter.

- **Correct location?** Some business venues look much like another and you can waste hours looking for them. Are you at the right event? It sounds elementary, I know. But some conference suites have similar sounding names. It is possible to find yourself being directed to the wrong group of delegates!
- **Be punctual** – a late arrival doesn't convey the best impression.
- Remember to **take your business cards** with you. It saves scribbling on the back of envelopes or train tickets.
- If for some reason you arrive early – don't worry. **Get involved**. Ask the organisers if there's some way in which you can help. It will give you something to do and take your mind off how nervous you are.

A tip I was once given by a leading QC was that if you get to a venue early, find out where the loos are. If anyone asks you, you can direct them with confidence. It gives the impression that you are familiar with the location and will boost your self-assurance!

And finally, wasn't it Woody Allen who said, '80% of success is turning up'?

PREPARE YOURSELF

- **Be positive and outwardly confident** – it will make you stand out above others. Don't worry if you have butterflies, research shows that over 90% of people feel fear about walking into a room full of strangers.

- Avoid arriving with coats, bags, umbrellas and other paraphernalia. Leave belongings at the cloakroom so you can **appear calm, unflustered** and unencumbered. Remember, you are judged in the first fifteen seconds of meeting someone. You don't want to blow your opportunity.

- **Rehearse entering the room**. Pause on the threshold and look around. Don't head straight for the bar. Take a few deep breaths. This will calm you down and give you a moment to recall your strategy.

- **Smile** – it signals confidence and openness.

- If you enter the room alone, **look for other people** standing on their own and make an approach. The chances are that they are feeling awkward, too. Striking up a conversation with them will show that you care about others and are not preoccupied with yourself. It will help them feel better about being there and you will have made a new friend already.

- **Practise your introduction on someone** beforehand – even if it is your dog! The stronger your greeting – the more memorable it is.

- **Try introducing yourself by your first name**. It is more informal and you will convey the impression of being approachable. You can begin by saying your name twice, as in 'Hello, my name's Bond, James Bond.'

- When introduced to someone, have a **firm handshake**. Try to avoid bone crunching, please. Have the name of your host or organisation at the ready. Know whose guest you are, or what group you are expected to join.

MAKING AN ENTRANCE

How you enter the room and engage people is very important.

- To make an impact, work on your **opening line**. This is often called a 'lift pitch'. Rehearse a sentence which summarises what anyone needs to know about what you do in thirty seconds.

- **Posture is important** – stand up straight. At business functions you should always be alert and attentive.

- Look around the room for acquaintances or **friendly faces**. This doesn't mean grabbing a colleague and cowering in a corner with them for the rest of the evening, avoiding everyone else.

- Maintain **appropriate eye contact**. Avoid staring, glaring, winking, blinking or looking straight over people's shoulders to others beyond.

- **Stay relaxed** – gripping the stem of your wine glass until it breaks isn't a smart idea.

- Develop good rapport by asking a non-threatening question. **Open questions** are best rather than something that is likely to produce a yes/no answer. Even an enquiry as simple as 'How far did you have to travel to get here?' opens the conversational gambit.

- **Be animated**. This can be simply a matter of varying the your vocal tone. A demonstration of your limbo-dancing skills is not necessary!

- **Find a way to 'hook' your audience**. If you propose to use humour – watch out for 'political correctness'. You can charm people by being sincerely interested in them and listening to what they say.

THINGS TO WATCH OUT FOR

While there are quite a few 'dos', there are also some things (and people) that it's best to steer clear of:

- If you can, **avoid contact with potential troublemakers**, such as, for example, the person who's had too much to drink and wants you to give them a lift home.

- It's best not to lecture people or use emotive gestures, however passionately you may feel about the subject under discussion. **Don't be aggressive** or speak with force. This is not Parliament or Speakers' Corner.

- Decisive people don't dither. If you find yourself in awkward company and you want to make a discreet exit from the group, prepare yourself. Become the master of the **graceful withdrawal**. Make your excuse politely but firmly. Say 'I'm sorry, but I see my colleague is about to leave and I must speak to him.'

- By all means eat the delicious food that's being handed round but **don't eat and talk at the same time**. It's difficult to engage in meaningful conversation

with someone whose mouth is full. Equally, if you
are eating when you're asked a question, wait until
you've finished before replying. No one likes being
showered with crumbs and particles of food.

◆ **Rapport is a two-way thing**. Dominating people often
monopolise conversations with loud, uninteresting
details about themselves. Withdraw with tact and
dignity. In the same way, if you've tried several
opening gambits and have been met by a blank stare
and monosyllabic answers, it's time to move on.

◆ **Beware** the predatory person whose sole purpose is
to meet and attempt to date attractive fellow guests.
(This warning is non-gender specific.) Also watch out
for limpets, the nervous types who, having
earmarked you as friendly, stick to you throughout
the evening and are impossible to shake off.

HOW TO BE MEMORABLE

One of the major aims of the exercise is to make
connections, but if those connections can't recall who
you are, it isn't any benefit to you.

◆ By being polite and courteous, you will be
unforgettable. Go on a **charm offensive**. Deal with
people kindly and sympathetically. Offer to fetch
someone a drink, or introduce a stranger into your
group.

◆ Take pride in what you do and be professional.
Whatever the occasion, you never know who you
might meet. Keeping a **conversational tone** to your

voice encourages people to respond to you in a friendly manner.

◆ **Speak slowly and clearly**. So often in modern venues there is loud background noise because of the lack of soft-furnishings. Conversations are hard to maintain above this level of sound, so speak in a way that makes it easier for others to hear what you have to say.

◆ You need not feel insignificant when talking to others who are more brilliant or experienced than yourself. Remember emotional intelligence stands out way beyond paper qualifications. Develop **the swan technique** – keep a calm exterior and smooth behaviour. No one can see what's going on beneath the waterline.

◆ Try to **establish connections** with people. This comes naturally with practice. Have you both recently been on holiday? Do you come from a particular region/ country? If there are some wallflowers, seek them out by asking if they have seen the host/hostess. You may be equally shy but it will help you overcome your nerves.

Some common pitfalls to avoid
It's equally important to avoid being remembered for the wrong reasons.

◆ **Avoid clumsy exit lines** – try, 'I've taken up enough of your time. I really mustn't monopolise you any longer.' Watch your body language and gestures.

Don't rush – tension is easily communicated.

- If you have a time limit, **be polite** and excuse yourself with tact. If you have a tendency towards the 'butterfly' technique – slow down. You can't speak to everyone in the room, so there's no point in trying.

- Make **appropriate eye contact** so as not to unnerve your companion. The eye dart – looking at a person for less than two seconds before your gaze flicks elsewhere – is most unsettling. The opposite – the fixed unblinking stare – is just as bad. Also avoid 'mowing the lawn' – looking from one side of the room to the other. It is disconcerting for those in your group, as well as being impolite.

- Check those **annoying habits**. However tense you may be, playing with your hair, fiddling with jewellery or tie (your own or someone else's) is not acceptable. Any hand-wringing, twitching or fidgeting is vastly irritating to watch.

- For those who are particularly nervous it may sound simple but **don't forget to breathe**! This simple relaxation technique is often overlooked. Most experienced actors and public speakers practise deep breathing before going out on stage. What works for them will work for you.

- If you are bored, **don't sit down**. It's too easy to get trapped that way or you may just appear unapproachable.

- Use light-hearted anecdotes as conversation fillers,

but always **be sensitive** to other people's feelings. Also consider this when initiating a conversation by asking a question. Make sure the question is innocuous.

◆ If you **mind has gone blank** ask for someone's business card on the pretext of giving it to another guest by way of introduction. Repeat their name a couple of times to (hopefully) fix it in your mind.

◆ Respect other people's **personal space** – stand about one metre away from people you don't know well. Body language will indicate if and when it's safe to approach more closely!

Some conversational tips

Try teaming up with a colleague. The buddy system helps to get round the room more effectively, particularly if it is a large gathering. Ask your host to help if there is someone you specifically want to meet. They can arrange to introduce you.

Have a trivial, little-known fact to trigger interest if conversation flags.

If you use your three best opening gambits and still have made little progress, **prepare to move on**.

Watch others in action and emulate those you admire. You can always learn from any situation, however experienced you are. If someone else's actions make you cringe with embarrassment at least you've seen how not to do something.

Keeping your eyes and ears open to what is going on around you heightens awareness.

When moving from group to group around the room **do so with purpose but in a controlled manner**. You'll be surprised how many people will notice you.

Allow your voice to have expression when you chat. Warmth and confidence encourage responses in others.

However fascinating you may find one person, **don't ignore the rest of your group**. Encourage others to talk about themselves or their interests.

Use pauses for effect. Never underestimate the power of silence. You will have your companions' undivided attention – at least for a few seconds!

Don't interrupt when someone else is speaking, however witty the comment you want to make. This is rude and alienates people.

Networking is fun

Remember to enjoy yourself, the venue and the hospitality. After all, this is supposed to be a social occasion, even though it is work-related. Be entertaining (within reason) – again this does not require limbo dancing and the like.

Mix with the other guests. Don't get glued to one spot or stick to one group.

Move outside your own comfort zone – be brave. You never know who you might meet. If there is someone you particularly want to meet, make contact at some point during the event. Even if they are about to leave – hand them your card and ask for their email address. Never miss an opportunity if you can help it.

Enthusiasm is catching. Being positive is attractive. It helps shyness evaporate and will get you noticed, but stay in control – watch the alcohol consumption.

If you are anxious to break into a closely-knit group who seem reluctant to split, you could take a plate of food and offer it to them. Then stay with them. This can go wrong if you happen to be dressed in black and white at the time (as has happened to me). You may be mistaken for one of the catering staff!

Ways to handle awkward situations

If you make an embarrassing social gaffe, have the courage to admit the fault and apologise. Being upfront and honest can turn a mistake to your advantage.

Avoid a difficult question by asking someone else's view. You could even turn the question round and ask the person posing the question for their response. When you have listened to their reply it may help your own reaction.

If someone drops a bombshell they may be testing your response. Rather than give them the satisfaction of erupting, try to suspend reaction. A measured acknowledgement buys you time and can save faces and reputations.

Making a tactical and diplomatic withdrawal from a potentially explosive situation is sometimes the only way to avoid disaster. Have an escape route handy, such as, 'I've just seen my host beckoning to me – please excuse me, I must go.'

If you are forced to listen to gossip, steer clear of getting involved in the discussion. Do not get drawn into conversation. Offer advice only when specifically asked for it. No one likes a know-it-all.

REAPING THE REWARDS

There are lots of rewards, and things to remember about how to collect them. The more you attend networking events, the easier it becomes. Your social skills become second nature to you. Continually practise wherever you are – in the supermarket, at the gym, when travelling.

Join other organisations where you can shine and radiate confidence. New members are often welcomed in groups – take advantage of every opportunity.

Devise ways of being of value to others. Offer to **share your contacts** and skills with them. Ask them to reciprocate. Pay attention to each new personal connection you make. Show interest in them, sincerely, by following-up shortly after your meeting.

Be curious – ask questions (but not personal or sensitive ones). Develop a genuine interest in other people. To build trust takes time. Don't expect overnight results.

Take contact details of everyone you meet. Make sure you have an effective way of **keeping notes**. This is your unique contacts database. Your memory – however good it is – will fail you sometimes.

Make regular **telephone call follow-ups**. It's not as daunting as you think. Call people even when you don't want anything from them. They will be amazed – and they will remember you. Keep a smile in your voice – it shows!

UNDERSTANDING THE PROCESS

Networking is essential – it is important to build internal and external contacts. Networking builds rapport with bosses, subordinates and peers. It also fosters relationships with customers, suppliers and competitors.

Networking and selling, however, are like chalk and cheese. Networking events should be used as a platform to make positive business connections. You may sell yourself, but not your products or services. There is much to be gained professionally and personally from networking inside and outside your company.

At its best, networking is a process of making connections with a diverse range of people. These connections can then be developed into reciprocal relationships to increase your business or advance your career.

One of the reasons why networking gets a bad name is because people who do not understand the process abuse it by trying to sell services or products. Meeting people who do not respect your values and attitudes, who have poor interpersonal skills and who find it difficult to share, can be off-putting.

If you've encountered people who go to an event unprepared, have low self-esteem and fear rejection, they require careful handling. Through shyness, their persona and approach are negative. They lack self-confidence and show no sign of curiosity about others because they are too wrapped up in themselves.

Conversely, those who miss the point of networking creatively will attempt to dominate groups and conversations. They will not engage in dialogue nor show any interest in offering help to others.

By keeping the positive benefits firmly in mind – you will find the process an enjoyable precursor to the next stages of building brilliant business connections.

SUMMARY

◆ Everyone needs to network, whether it is for jobs, information or fresh ideas.

◆ **Have a plan**. If you know what your goals are you'll be able to work out who you need to meet to get there.

◆ **Analyse your network**. Who do you already know and how well do you know them?

◆ **Don't assume the most senior people are the most valuable** – pay attention to juniors and admin staff, too.

◆ **Attend selected events**. You can't be everywhere and you don't need to be.

◆ **Image is important** – don't be too formal or too scruffy.

◆ **Be organised**. When you collect details make a note of them and follow up with information that is relevant to your contacts.

- **Be consistent** – do make time for contacting people. If you are persistent the rewards are high.

4

The Three-Stage Plan: Step Two – Making Connections

'We should give as we would receive, cheerfully, quickly, and without hesitation; for there is no grace in a benefit that sticks to the fingers.'
Seneca: 4BC–65AD, Roman Philosopher

In the previous chapter, we covered effective networking skills. You've attended events and collected the names of potential contacts. Now, how do you turn these into brilliant business connections?

It's time to set out your objectives, understand and document your goals.

MAINTAINING A SYSTEM

Who have you recently met, or who is already in your database, that you want to build connections with? You will be able to start quite simply. Focus on success and the business development you will achieve.

Begin by identifying common links and themes to each and everyone in your database.

TIP

Maintain a system – it always helps to be organised. You have your database – how clean is it?

With practice you can usually find two or three things in common within a few minutes. Use this as the common ground from which to build a valuable connection.

If you're a keen gardener and you buy some new plants, the first thing you'd probably do is set about the border in which you're going to put them. It's an ideal opportunity to create some space – remove the weeds and trim the existing shrubs that haven't been tended for the last six months.

This analogy may seem a bit incongruous when contrasted to the tough business world we're writing about, but it works!

When you consider your database – cleanliness is definitely next to godliness. If your contacts are moth-eaten, out of date, choked and surrounded by dead wood, there's no way you'll be able to optimise their worth. Add potentially new and exciting contacts to this, and they will get swamped by the old material and will sink without trace within a short space of time.

The information you should be aiming to record on your business connections includes:

- the contact's name, address, telephone number, fax and email

- their company name and job title

- the source of the original meeting, venue or person who introduced you

- a record of what transpired at the first meeting

- the type of person/reaction – cold/tepid, warm/hot

- the arrangement for follow-up – timing/method

- any personal details – birthday/family/hobbies and interests

- geographical details – the area of country if you are visiting them

- background – them/their company/previous positions held

- their and your aims and objectives, links and mutual acquaintances.

Spending some time on a database cleanse and update not only refreshes your memory as to what's in it, but helps you work out which contacts will connect well with your new acquaintances. From here you can begin to create even more exciting and harmonious relationships which you can develop with your newly acquired skills.

Attitudes and approaches

One of the categories listed above may seem slightly
unusual to you, but I find it helpful when measuring the
level of my response to people. There are four degrees
of reaction when you meet someone for the first time.

Type 1: assertive–cold

These people do not trust new contacts. They are
introverted and do not welcome approaches from other
people. They prefer to remain aloof. It will not be easy
to penetrate their reserve.

Do not expect a warm welcome when you meet them.
Accept their negative attitude – it is not personal. Use
your professionalism as a foil. Keep small talk to an
absolute minimum and emphasise that you are talking
to them for sound business reasons. Make your opening
remarks short and very much to the point.

Type 2: accommodating–cold

These people are a little warmer than Type 1. The best
way is to let them take the lead. Demonstrate that you
are in control of the interview by attentive listening,
note taking and asking concise, factual and open
questions. These will help to direct the meeting. Be firm,
polite but never subservient. Position yourself as
confident, professional and calmly determined.

Type 3: accommodating–warm

You can expect a warm welcome, but so can everyone
else. Their warmth does not indicate that you are

particularly special. Allow them to express their feelings with some small talk but stay in control. Do not lose sight of the fact that you are there for business reasons.

These people like to think they belong to select groups so mention as early as possible the involvement you or your company have with other comparable, reputable companies. Tell them how you would like to progress the relationship, including your role and theirs.

Do not be too business-like and officious. Keep the opening conversational and flexible. Position yourself as a friendly contact.

Type 4: assertive–warm

Expect a correct and professional opening with a warm handshake.

Be as professional as you can, this person will expect you to acknowledge them as commercially astute. Your opening remarks should be short and clearly indicate the purpose behind the meeting.

Flexibility is the key so that their ideas can be accommodated in a joint desire for the business relationship to progress. Be prepared to review your objectives and avoid standard approaches or responses.

Review – little and often is best
The best thing to do is a quarterly or half-yearly update of your database.

Check your closest contacts first to ensure that their details have not changed. If someone has been promoted, make sure that you have a note of their correct job title. Your valuable contact will not be pleased at being addressed as 'Senior Associate' when he or she has just been made up to director level. Any misinformation that remains uncorrected works against agreeable business relationships.

Make a note in your diary to update your contacts on a regular basis. If you do this carefully it won't become a mammoth task. This will lessen the risk of the job being put off to an indefinite date.

Who really is who?
At the same time, review the structure of your network of contacts. Are they categorised correctly so that it is possible to access people quickly?

Do you have enough groups, categories and sub-sections?
Client, prospect, supplier is okay but it won't really be sufficiently detailed. You could include clubs, organisations, profession, industry, sector. Imagine you're attending a conference in Bristol next month. Can you find, at the press of a button, all the business contacts you have in that geographical area? Do you have time to organise visits to them or entertain them while you are there?

Create whatever fields you need so that you have the information readily accessible at your fingertips. Keep the notes section updated each time you make contact or meet.

A SYSTEMATIC APPROACH

When you have a systematic approach to keeping your contacts list neat, clean and tidy, you'll use it more often and effectively. Self-discipline and orderly procedures make it a valuable accessory.

Set up a monthly reminder note to contact anyone you haven't seen or spoken to in the last six to eight weeks. They will appreciate you keeping in touch. A friendly enquiry as to how they are may be all that's required. Many people will be amazed that you've rung them without any particular reason or ulterior motive attached.

KEY POINT

It's worth repeating something that's already been mentioned: building long-term, trusting and respectful relationships takes time – not only in personal matters but also in business. If you rush it you will be disappointed.

Developing connections with like-minded people with whom you can do business, either now or in the future, is the aim. One of the best ways that works is to try to help them as much as they can help you.

When working to create brilliant business connections, don't compartmentalise your contacts too rigidly. Links between people are unplanned and spontaneous. (It could be something as simple as discovering that you both worked for the same company some years previously.) Coincidences often occur and by avoiding boundaries and boxes you will be open to every opportunity as it presents itself.

QUALITY VERSUS QUANTITY

If you put into practice the suggestions I've already made, you should be building and strengthening an effective and valuable collection of contacts which is regularly refreshed and added to.

Keep lines of communication clean and clear and use your network to develop new and exciting lines of approach. It is better to have a smaller and more manageable collection of contacts than something large, unwieldy and inaccurate.

APPLIED THINKING

Who are you looking for and how do you put your contacts to work? Are you are considering moving to another job within your company? How can your database help you?

For a start, it would be sensible to speak to people who are already working in that department or who have held a similar post elsewhere. As well as your peer group, consider talking to junior staff. They will have a different 'take' on the organisation which could be useful.

Look at the situation from all possible angles. Who do you know who could give you advice or information? Think laterally as well as upwards and downwards.

You could consider finding someone who would act as a possible mentor. They may be older and more experienced and have adopted a similar approach some years previously and guide you towards meeting your goals.

CATEGORISING YOUR BUSINESS CONNECTIONS

Why do you network? What activities do you pursue? Where do you do it?

Everyone in your database is a business connection. This includes existing clients, prospects, former clients, suppliers, influencers, bridges, links and gatekeepers. It can also include those with whom you work, former colleagues, past employees, ex-employers. Beyond that it reaches members of your clubs, professional associations, associated businesses and other networks. It can also include your friends and acquaintances.

> **KEY POINT**
>
> Anyone serious about building brilliant business connections has to be focused on what they want to achieve.

How you make use of these connections depends on what you want to achieve and what activities you pursue.

Be selective
It's impossible to keep in touch with everybody you meet, and it's not necessary to do so.

There comes a time when people move on and you lose touch. But with good organisation and an effective network you can maintain a link with these contacts through mutual third parties.

You'll probably know how effective this is if you've used networks such as Friends Reunited. By maintaining contact with, say, only three friends from school days, you can get linked to many others who attended the same educational establishment at roughly the same time.

There are numerous websites now that offer networked links from one group of professionals to others. This is a fairly quick, effective and safe way of increasing your contacts. It's positive proof of the rule of 'Six Degrees of Separation'.

The idea of Six Degrees of Separation was devised by the American social psychologist, Stanley Milgram in the 1960s. His original experiment, using posted letters forwarded from person to person, suggested most people are connected to each other through a chain of about six acquaintances. (The 1993 film *Six Degrees of Separation*, starring Donald Sutherland and Will Smith, was inspired by this research.)

Apparently, the small world phenomenon is not only real now but far more universal than most people think. Scientists want to research further to provide answers to such questions as how ideas spread, why fashions come and go, how a small failure can cause catastrophic global consequences (either scientifically or financially).

The fact that the Six Degrees rule works helps to explain why, amongst many things, complete strangers often turn out to have mutual friends and why gossip can spread so quickly. The press often contains reports on the way electronic messages (particularly ones of dubious sexual content) spread like wildfire across the world within hours, causing acute embarrassment to the unfortunate sender.

But one important factor in all this is motivation. If you lose interest in the process, everything falls apart.

If apathy prevails, nothing will happen. There has to be an incentive to continue to build your network, increase your contacts base and develop business relationships. This comes down to your own personal attitude.

SUGGESTED METHODS OF CONNECTING

Some people host networking events, others belong to a selected number of professional associations and attend their meetings regularly.

You can use a number of opportunities, such as receptions, parties, industry-related conferences, seminars and workshops. Attending exhibitions, professional interest group workshops, private social functions and sport and leisure events are also useful.

There is limitless opportunity these days to meet people and foster good connections, but it's only with persistence that the relationships will flourish. You can't become 'best friends' with someone by putting in sporadic appearances every six months!

Whatever you do, wherever you feel most comfortable, be alert and open to making connections.

The difference between 'networking' and 'connecting' is that there is more than one common thread running throughout.

In addition to your profession, the event at which you are both present, or the fact that you have been introduced through a mutual friend or colleague, you probably have other links in common.

Coincidences do occur

Recently a friend invited me to attend a reception. Unfortunately on that particular evening, illness prevented my friend from attending, but he suggested I went along anyway. I did what a lot of people dread, and walked into a room full of strangers. The first person who spoke to me was (like everyone else in the room) totally unknown to me.

To break the ice, I asked him what he did. He said he'd retired last year from a career in teaching. I enquired as to where he'd taught and he named a few schools, one of which I recognised. I told him that a friend of mine was teaching there. He was amazed. My friend and this man had been colleagues for over 25 years and he'd been best man at his wedding. It *is* a small world!

New approaches

Invest some time in polishing up your existing network. Work out where your new contacts fit in, and how they dovetail with your existing contacts.

Spend time working out how best to categorise and detail them. Think about whether they are decision-makers, influencers, bridges, links or gatekeepers.

- A **decision-maker** is someone who can award contracts and has the power to agree to something you want to happen.

- **An influencer**'s word carries weight if he mentions you to the decision maker – sometimes called a recommender.

- A **bridge** is someone who can introduce you to another person you want to contact who you can't otherwise reach.

- A **link** is a mutual connection between you and someone else which helps establish credibility and trust with the new person – not to be confused with name dropping.

- A **gatekeeper** is the person that stands between you and your desired contact – always be extra nice to them.

It used to be a rule in the early days of my career that young men were told 'always be nice to young women – you never know who they might marry'.

This is rather out of date (and shows my age) but the advice is still relevant. In today's world of ever-changing jobs and faster communication, it pays to be respectful and polite to everyone wherever possible. Someone you meet today could so easily turn up in six months' time at another location or organisation. If they remember you, they could perhaps influence someone favourably on your behalf.

Decide who belongs in which category, where the gaps are and how you are going to set about filling them.

Consider who can help you to do this and what you can offer them in return.

To assist you, here are a few A words to consider:

- How should I **approach** people?
- My **aim** to communicate **appropriately**.
- **Asking** – enquire first and then listen.
- Develop an **attitude** of gratitude.
- What **action** should I take?
- Offer **assistance** and ask for help.
- When enquiring about something be **attentive** and **aware**.
- Keep **alert** to the possibilities of **alliances** which can **add** value.
- Learn to **appreciate** others and their **abilities**.
- **Analyse** situations to your own **advantage**.
- Be **adaptable** to other people's needs.

THE CASE FOR DEVELOPING BUSINESS CONNECTIONS

There is no doubt, close connections in business save time and money. Business effectiveness depends more on human-related activities – relationships, interpersonal skills and communication – than on technical skills and abilities. So how do you identify the best business connections?

Anyone is potentially a good connector, but they must understand what you offer or need. If you don't take the time to explain this to them, how can they possibly help you, or vice versa? This is why, when you encounter someone with whom you feel 'rapport', make sure you get a half hour meeting with them shortly afterwards to follow-up.

You need to spend some quality time with a new contact fairly early on in the process, to establish how best you can help each other. It could be that one of you is new to the company you work for, so you could want information on who is who and how things are done.

Alternatively, you could be looking for information or researching a particular subject on which this person is an expert. If so, consider ways in which you can be of use to them.

People who are skilled at developing brilliant business connections integrate the process into their lives. They have wide-ranging contacts with whom they keep in constant touch. They exchange ideas, information and offer help. You probably recall meeting such people. Maybe you are one of them.

Their outstanding characteristics include sincerity, curiosity, consideration, sharing, understanding and appreciation. They are the 'givers' rather than 'takers'. They keep in touch with their contacts even though there is seemingly 'nothing in it for them'. They are always open to opportunities to assist people and to broaden their network by sharing connections.

Reasons to get started

If you want to turn your contacts into connections, you need to work at cementing relationships. This is done simply by getting to know people better. Make the time and opportunity for face-to-face meetings whenever possible. Early on in the process, one-to-one meetings are best. They help to build rapport quickly and easily. Further on in the relationship it is often helpful to include other interested parties.

The responsibility for getting communication right lies firmly with the communicator. Clarity and appropriateness are important.

Checking your intentions is also vital. Why am I doing this? What is your response? It should be accurate – if it is vague, have a rethink.

Ask yourself these questions:

◆ What does my new business contact need to know?

◆ How much detail should I give them?

◆ What sort of action do I want to have as a result of this exchange?

◆ How is it to be done?

◆ How do I want them to feel – in agreement, pleased, enthusiastic?

If you are clear as to why something is being done, and you have set yourself defined objectives, then plan how you are going to deliver the message.

◆ Is significant feedback necessary? If so, it should be handled by a face-to-face meeting.

◆ Is some simple feedback necessary? Possibly a phone conversation will suffice.

◆ Does complexity require a combination of both methods?

In each situation a number of different factors will influence the chosen method: urgency, complexity, formality, involvement of a number of other parties etc.

Every possible method of approach needs to be considered. Choice should be made with regard to such criteria and avoid the temptation to do what is easiest (for example, just sending an email)!

Most of you have doubtless spent hours of your precious time in pointless gatherings where little useful information is exchanged or discussed. If you have a dislike of meetings, you will be aware of the

If you choose a face-to-face meeting, remember they may not be everyone's favourite activity.

need for a planned approach.

Meetings are simply a form of communication which can be used to:

- inform
- analyse and solve problems
- discuss and exchange views
- inspire and motivate
- counsel and reconcile conflict
- obtain opinion and feedback
- persuade
- reinforce the status quo
- instigate change in knowledge, skills or attitudes.

Meetings are potentially useful and are essential in the relationship-building process. It is only by continued contact can you reach a close rapport with someone.

Use your meetings wisely:

- Keep people informed and up to date.
- Provide a chance to be heard.
- Create involvement with others.
- Use marketing as a social gathering to allow cross-functional contact.
- Provide personal visibility.
- Also use them to broaden experience and promote exchange of ideas.

Getting your face-to-face meeting off to a good start involves responsibility. If you are being proactive in creating a close relationship with someone who could be vitally important to your career or business development plans, remember these points:

- Make the meeting positive.
- Ensure its purpose is clear.
- Establish your authority and engage the other person.
- Create the right atmosphere – friendly and flexible.
- Generate interest and enthusiasm for the process.
- Be professional and businesslike but informal.
- Keep to time limits – respect other people's schedules.

A well-run meeting demands concentration. You should avoid interruptions and make the process effective in the following ways:

- Actively stimulate creative thinking.
- Contribute new ideas and encourage others to do the same.
- Steer the discussion into new or unusual directions.
- Find new ways of looking at things.
- Consider novel approaches and give them a chance.
- Aim to overcome obstacles to progress.

Communication is a two-way process, and there'll be more on this later. If you want to stimulate feedback, comment, exchange of ideas and suggestions, you should positively encourage it. To ensure your business relationship starts well, encourage communication with your new contact.

- Create a culture where two-way communication is expected.

- Stimulate it by regularly keeping in touch by a variety of means.

- Make it easy – provide feedback and useful pieces of information.

- React positively to each and every exchange – acknowledge and thank them.

- Give credit – this will ensure a flow of ideas and exchanges.

- Make time to do this on a regular basis however busy you are.

- Be available when your business contact makes an approach.

Finally, keep the possibilities for creating a proactive relationship in mind. Encourage the process, be versatile and flexible to keep your contact's attention. For example, don't just 'do lunch'. Invite your new contact to a variety of different events. A business breakfast is a good way of keeping in touch and not spending a lot of time 'catching up'. Much progress can be made in an hour before the working day starts.

If your contact is an evening person, rather than an early starter, meet for a drink after work. A 'happy hour' approach is informal and relaxed and can work wonders if that is a comfortable way of connecting for both of you.

Whichever method of approach you use, make sure it is a continuous process. Set aside a proportion of your working week for connection making and relationship-building and you will be amazed at the results.

Following up on a face-to-face meeting can often best be done in writing. If this is what you propose to do, try to be:

- ◆ concise (as brief as content and purpose allow)
- ◆ understandable (avoiding ambiguity)
- ◆ precise (saying what is necessary and no more)
- ◆ in plain language (without jargon or technical terms)
- ◆ simple (in language and grammatical structure)
- ◆ descriptive (letting your words add to the message).

When there's no 'reason' to meet, keep in touch remotely. You can phone, email or write. Use the opportunity to carry out some research, gather market knowledge, exchange ideas or share contacts.

While you are being generous with your time and connections, your business contact will be busy trying to reciprocate. You'll earn respect and your reputation will be enhanced. In addition you'll make more new friends and have a good time.

Natural business connectors have certain things in common:

- They treat everyone as being interesting, special and likeable.

- They use good eye contact and positive body language.

- They make other people, particularly new acquaintances, feel safe and part of the occasion.

- They introduce people to each other effortlessly, remembering names and something relevant about those they introduce.

In a word, they have 'charisma'.

Go on a charm offensive

Have you met someone like this? When you were introduced, they smiled, entered into conversation easily and drew you out? They probably asked you questions about yourself, and listened to what you said. They made you feel important. When you parted, you probably thought to yourself, 'What a great person!'

Not only is it easy to be in their company, they are at ease with themselves.

Am I describing someone you know, or am I describing the person you want to be?

Charm is contagious. To be a charmer, you should be assertive but not arrogant, vain or conceited. Charmers are confident and they build self-esteem in others. They have broad horizons, are not narrow minded and are enthusiastic. Above all, they are curious, asking lots of questions. They empathise, are responsive, have a great sense of humour and are frequently self-deprecating. They are at ease using a number of different communication styles and often employ 'mirroring' techniques. And, they know how to listen!

MASTERING THE ART OF GOOD QUESTIONS

This is perhaps the single most powerful interpersonal tool in building business connections. A good question is one which shows you are interested in the other person. It's an open question – requiring more of an answer than just 'yes' or 'no'.

KEY POINT

Good questions build great relationships. It indicates that you care about the other person and their situation. The more questions you ask, the more you are encouraging that person to trust you.

Good questions convey competence, sincerity and sympathy. You should practise the art of listening too. By paying attention to what people say, you can note this information for future use. If you greet someone the next time you meet by asking them how they enjoyed their holiday in Antigua, (assuming that it was their holiday destination) you'll rise high in their estimation.

SUMMARY

Seven steps for making connections

You've networked to make connections. You now recognise the crucial differences between networking and connecting. Let's look at how we make connections again.

1 Database

Hopefully, you've designed and customised your business network architecture (the database). The next step is to audit existing and past connections. You have noted the relationships that are still valuable or potentially useful, and added all the new information you've collected.

2 Categories

Have you designated each contact an appropriate category – cross-referencing where necessary?

Now you are looking to link your contacts together. Start by connecting individuals where there are possible collaborations, complementary skills and services, potential partnerships and alliances.

At this point you are in a position to help your contacts by sharing connections to win, retain and develop their careers or business. Internally, within your company, you're aware of the importance of relationship-building, empowering individuals and teams. You're ready to facilitate connections between employees, employers and other influencers to deliver outstanding results.

3 Links

With practice you'll be aware of the skills required to handle delicate issues, where sensitive business connections and confidentiality are paramount. You will also be noting which people would be best positioned to assist you when these opportunities arise.

4 Keep in touch

It always pays dividends to let your contacts know that you consider them special and worthy of particular value. That alone can set you apart from others, particularly those who do not understand the benefits of one-to-one attention.

Don't forget that when one of your contacts leaves a company, you have diverging paths. Not only do you want to keep in touch with your friend in his new position, but you will also want to start a rapport with his successor. So many people fail to track their contacts when they relocate and waste a valuable resource by doing so.

By establishing and maintaining communication with your contacts on a regular basis, you are putting yourself ahead of many people. You will earn respect, encourage trust and add value to the relationship you are nurturing and developing. Keep your connections warm and friendly. People naturally gravitate towards those who they feel will be empathetic. Pay attention to your contacts' needs and wants, and when the time comes, let them know how you can help.

5 Note worthy

If you make a habit of detailing information, it will pay off in spades. By this I mean keeping notes of meetings, exchanges, telephone conversations, etc. Within a few months you'll most likely be able to offer something relevant to their needs.

No matter how tenuous the link, your contacts will register the fact that you remembered them. Irrespective of whether the moment has passed and they no longer need that contact or service, it will emphasise to them that you really were listening.

6 Be distinctive

It's not hugely important what you do to make yourself stand apart from the pack as long as you do it. Grandiose plans for luxurious and expensive corporate entertaining packages to leading social events are not necessary and neither are they what I am talking about.

What works best is something that is affordable, attainable and relatively easy to offer. If you have access to information which could be advantageous to your contacts, offer it to them. You may have some sporting interests in common, or facilities which they could use, in which case invite them to participate.

I try to invite my contacts to events which I think would interest them, or bring them into contact with new people who they might not otherwise meet. Often it encourages them to be more adventurous and experience pastures new. If they enjoy the experience, and meet rewarding and stimulating company, they will be happy to do something for you in return.

Whatever method you employ, to be distinguishable in business is a great form of advertising. It speaks volumes not only for you personally, but also your company.

Proactivity

By being proactive in engaging with your contacts, you will be setting yourself and your company apart from its competitors. Remembering people's names and personal details may seem unimportant, but even the smallest nugget of information can keep you in the forefront of a contact's mind.

Establishing yourself as an 'identity' means that your contacts will remember you ahead of other people they have in their data base. Be outstanding, and they'll go out of their way to help you and your business.

To recap:

♦ **Networking is the essential first stage.** It is the frame or skeleton.

♦ **Making connections is the second step**, putting flesh on to the bone and developing the frame.

♦ **The third and final stage, building relationships**, is where you breathe life into the process. That is when the muscles on the frame are made to work.

5

The Three-Stage Plan: Step 3 – Relationship-Building

> Friendship is constant in all other things, save
> in the office and affairs of love.
> *William Shakespeare,* Much Ado about Nothing

Here comes the difficult bit! How do you build deep, meaningful business relationships?

There's no easy answer to this, neither is there a quick fix. However, there are a few important points to bear in mind before going on to develop the best strategy to suit your own purposes.

A TWO-WAY PROCESS

Any business relationship is a two-way process. The person with whom you are dealing will want to feel:

- important and respected
- his needs are considered
- he is able to trust you
- he wants your input and ideas to help him
- he will be advised in advance of any snags or problems.

This may sound a bit of a tall order, but until you have convinced your new business contact that you are professional, reliable, discreet and honest, the relationship will not proceed far.

You need to develop some self-awareness, too. Self-awareness enables you to be genuine.

It may be impossible ever to know yourself completely, but if you are trying to build good relationships with other people, being aware of your own personal strengths, weaknesses, hang-ups and prejudices is helpful to the process. What this means is awareness of your **attitudes and values**. If you are aware of these, you will then know how to adapt your own traits so that the relationship-building is not inadvertently hindered by your own behaviour.

GOOD INTENTIONS

Interacting between parties requires perception and sensitivity. Effective relationship-building is achieved by being alert in mind, emotion, body and spirit. Concentration levels need to be high.

You are starting a process of offering something to others in the hope of obtaining something in return. Confidence is a quality that springs from competence. People show confidence in different ways. Some are robust and self-assured. Others may be risk-takers and not daunted by challenging situations.

Keep an open mind. Every meeting with your business contacts will be unique and present different opportunities. If you are resourceful and adaptable, you won't need to have ready answers. What you are aiming for is to appear trustworthy and to be able to trust others in return.

WATCH YOUR STEP

The relationship-building process is like dancing. Each stage needs to be taken willingly and in tandem with the other party, before moving on to the next one.

If you are trying to lead your prospective contact on to the floor to do the tango, make sure he's not expecting to dance the waltz. Get your fancy footwork confused and you'll end up in a tangled heap on the floor which will be embarrassing for both parties.

> I remember asking a contact once what he felt we were achieving by pursuing our dialogue. He replied in exasperation, 'don't ask me the score – I don't even know what game we're playing!'.

Sometimes a pause will be required in between, to assess progress, and regroup. The process needs to be balanced – each party should be open in negotiations, able to weigh up the pros and cons of the information exchanged before making a decision to take a further step.

No relationship will be perfect, neither will it be easy or quick to achieve. In fact, the old saying 'more haste, less speed' is very apt. As long as a positive balance is maintained, progress will be made. The dance can sometimes be quite complex, depending upon the size and nature of your contact's business.

If the plan on your part is to move closer to an organisation where a major project is likely to be awarded, then the success or failure of the relationship you are attempting to build can be dramatically affected by a number of factors.

This could be other parties involved in the decision-making process, or competitors of yours who may also be lining up for favours.

As long as you remember that this process is inherently two-way, and that satisfaction is needed on both sides for it to continue, then you will be able to make progress towards a winning outcome.

In any complex process where there is a need to relate closely to someone, this can be done best if it is thought through carefully and approached in a planned and structured way. Effectively you are trying to play an influential part in the other side's decision-making process.

Your objective is to assist them to make decisions – the ones that will have the result of giving you the desired outcome. The more you are prepared to 'give' the more likely you are to achieve your goal.

KEEP ON TRACK

Your plan (or structured approach) needs to be like a map. Even if you have to deviate from the planned route, the chart should help you keep as close to your track as possible.

The overall process of relationship-building is multifaceted. It needs to be controlled and managed.

You will need to use ploys and gambits, as well as playing to your own unique strengths, to nurture the process. Try to keep in mind the importance of seeing things from the other side's point of view. Fine-tuning is paramount, so being able to deploy appropriate approaches from all your available interpersonal skills is advantageous.

A LEARNING CURVE

Learn something from every encounter, even if it's how not to do it in future!

If you are embarking on building brilliant business connections, you will probably be making hundreds of business development calls to your contacts every year, and arranging lots of meetings.

To maximise the advantage of the time you've spent doing this, get feedback. The amount of feedback available from these contacts is massive.

KEY POINT

Do you take advantage of this? Review your last six meetings or contact-building calls. Did you ask yourself:

- why did they say that
- did they misunderstand something I said
- why didn't they agree
- what did they really mean?

Try to get into the habit of reviewing each exchange in your mind after you've finished and analyse the results to improve your relationship-building the next time.

By adjusting the way you communicate with contacts you will avoid repeating your mistakes. Your overtures will appear fresh and well directed in future.

In business dealings, always prepare. Good planning is one way to give yourself a head start over any competitors.

Preparing yourself for your meeting with an important prospect could mean:

- just taking a few minutes of your time thinking matters through before you pick up the phone or start a meeting

- sitting round a table with a couple of colleagues discussing the best way to approach a key prospect.

Whatever method you use, make sure you always do it. Forewarned is forearmed.

If you are visiting someone who is very busy, the less of his time you take up will earn you points. Try to make the preamble fairly short – don't spend ten minutes explaining to him in minute detail what the traffic conditions were like on your journey.

On the other hand, if a 'warm-up' session is necessary to put your business contact at ease, spend a few minutes asking him about his golf handicap, or his most recent holiday. Be sensitive to his reactions.

Set objectives
If you don't know where you are going, how will you know when you get there? One way of looking at the relationship-building process is to regard it as starting out on a journey. Make sure you start from the best place!

Each exchange with every prospect needs clear objectives.

◆ Do you want to win new business?

◆ Do you want them to act as influencers or referrers for your company?

◆ Are you trying to obtain market information?

◆ Are you hoping to work for their organisation at some point?

◆ Do you want an introduction to a key decision-maker?

If you don't have a clear idea of what you are trying to achieve, it is difficult to set in motion the actions you need to achieve it.

Remember that well-known mnemonic attributable to so many business activities – when you are trying to build brilliant business connections, remember to work **SMART**.

◆ **Specific** – be clear about what you want to achieve.

◆ **Measurable** – identify the stages so you can track progress.

◆ **Achievable** – can you really do it? Be honest. Don't be over-ambitious.

◆ **Realistic** – should you actually start the relationship-building process. Is this the right time for you and your company?

◆ **Timed** – work out the timing. When do you expect to meet your objectives? In weeks, months or years?

MAKE IT A HABIT

Returning to the dancing analogy for a moment, consider your dance card. Ideally, you don't want to have any blank spaces on it, but neither do you want the same partner for each dance. It's absolutely true what they say about 'having all your eggs in one basket'. If you drop it, all you get is an omelette.

Balancing existing business relationships with finding new ones which you need to grow and nurture is a constant dilemma for anyone who wishes to progress. Some people find it almost impossible to free up the time required among other work priorities. To do justice to the importance of it, you must adopt a systematic and consistent approach.

What you are trying to avoid here is a 'feast and famine' scenario in your business where you either have too much to do or not enough. Business connections used wisely should alleviate the possibilities of this happening.

Another factor most people dread is 'cold prospecting'. If you nurture your contacts you should not have to tackle cold leads. All your connections – even the newest you are following – should be warm, if not actually hot.

If your plan is to provide a regular supply of interesting new projects, then the activity required to produce this stream of work should be carried out regularly and proactively. Make sure it is strategic and fits with your company's business development plans. New contacts are the lifeblood of most businesses, so make your first rule to be continually on the look out for new opportunities and connections; be systematic and persistent.

CREATING A METHOD

Whether you are looking for new business, information, or you're researching ideas, using one business contact to lead to another is a great way to continue to increase your sphere of influence.

One way of making this work is to ask your business contacts who else they would recommend you to talk to about the matter under discussion. You can ask them if you can mention their name. Provided you offer them something in return, they will most likely be generous in giving you the information.

Ask them who among your contacts it would be useful for them to meet, and make a point of following up on that request. Send them the information, invite them to the appropriate function, fix the next meeting, or introduce them to the third party at the next opportunity.

CENTRES OF INFLUENCE

There are people and organisations with whom you have made contact on a regular basis who have the power to influence or recommend. These could be trade and professional bodies, chambers of commerce, associations, financial institutions and other professional service firms.

By offering them some help or service, you will ensure they are reminded of what you do and are up to date on your company's activities.

Make a note of any business contact you have who could lead you to a number of other influential business people. If this reciprocal relationship is successful it is a most cost-effective and worthwhile way of increasing your network.

You can always win friends and influence people by offering to do some 'pro bono' work. This could be volunteering to give some of your professional expertise to a favourite charity or not-for-profit organisation, or to help fund-raise for a specific project.

Anything that emphasises your willingness to be a 'giver' rather than a 'taker' will get you noticed and remembered.

Chance contacts

Create opportunities by being observant. This sounds obvious but is often easily overlooked.

Scan your local paper, trade press, journals or professional publications. If you've recently read something about one of your business contacts, get in touch with them and say how pleased you were to see them mentioned in the news.

It could be that one of your contacts has just raised some money for a local hospital or charity. Maybe they, or their company, have won an award or a significant piece of new business. They will be flattered and remember that you took the time to call them.

> By being observant and showing your contact that you take an interest in them, they will remember you.

Don't ignore office gossip. You never know what you might learn! Maybe someone you know has moved into new premises across the road, or to the office suite on the floor above you. If they are on your contacts list, make a point of calling in to say hello.

Anything you can do to establish yourself in their mind will be helpful when trying to develop your business relationships.

Expect the unexpected

You never know when a chance encounter will provide a connection. If I had a fiver for every time I've struck up a conversation with a total stranger only to find we have at least three things in common within a few minutes of talking, I wouldn't be writing this book!

It doesn't always lead directly to work, but most times it has worked in my favour in some way or other. It could be as simple as being able to remark to one of your business contacts, 'You'll never guess who I met the other day. He said he's a great friend of yours ...'

When is the best time?

If you think that you should only make contact with people during working hours, you may be putting yourself at a disadvantage. Many professionals these days are expected to be available 24/7/365. I am not advocating this at all, but I do advise being around at times that suit the needs of your business contacts.

If the only time they can speak to you is at the weekend or after working hours, then it pays to be available and flexible. If you show that you're prepared to fit in with their timetable, it makes a lot of difference and can give you an advantage over others who do not.

This principle applies not only to contacting them but also to meeting them. Legend has it that many business deals have been struck on the golf course. There's no reason why it shouldn't work for you, too.

What to say

When it comes to making the call, or attending the meeting, with your business contact, be sure that you know your own business, and also theirs.

♦ Keep your checklist handy if you're unsure.

♦ Awareness of the objectives of your call or meeting is crucial to success.

♦ Have your key points ready for opening the dialogue.

♦ Be prepared to handle objections or overcome obstacles.

♦ Make a note of any actions or decisions that need to be made as a result of your discussions.

♦ Finally, emphasise the importance of your meeting by following-up afterwards and supplying information or offering services.

Think long-term

Rome wasn't built in a day, and neither were any good business relationships.

Good customer–client relationships are built over time and are therefore difficult to dislodge. If a relationship is based on secure foundations it will endure the hiccups and glitches that are inevitable in commercial transactions. New best friends started on the instant may be great for the moment, but be warned, they are frequently transitory. If they are built on shifting sand, they can disappear just as rapidly as they appeared.

If your industry or sector is prone to quiet times, it pays to stay in touch. Whatever your business or profession, it's not possible to be continuously involved in a

Being proactive with your business contacts while maintaining a positive mental attitude is essential. Be confident, polite and persistent.

working relationship. By keeping in contact when you are not engaged on a project, you will be the one who is remembered when things improve.

Make it personal
It's the thought that counts. You will get to know a great deal about someone over a period of time. Remembering a child's name or sending them a birthday card may seem trivial, but it will register that you are interested in them, not just the position they hold.

Also think of your business contacts when you meet new people. Introducing your contact to people who matter in their industry or profession will make them feel important. They will know that they are part of your inner circle of business connections. In turn they will be conscious that they owe you a favour in return.

Keep an ear to the ground
Listen to what they say. You can pick up clues about their hopes and fears and behave accordingly.

Equally, you might hear things about their organisation or industry from an unlikely source. Passing on news and pieces of information may help them avoid upsets and unwelcome surprises. They will appreciate the fact that you gave good advice or warned them of impending changes and will be keen to help you in return.

PERSISTENCE PAYS

To harness the power of personal connections you need to keep a few 'P' words in mind.

- **Persistence** pays, there's no doubt about that.

- Relationship-building is like **planting seeds** – they take time to germinate.

- One of the most important factors in the process is **preparation**.

- You need to prepare the ground. It pays to know about your **prospects**.

- You have to **persevere** – sometimes for months, and, in some cases, years.

- Try to be unfailingly **polite** and **patient**.

- A **positive** mental attitude and outlook is infectious.

- **Persuasive** tactics get easier with **practice**.

- Make sure you do some **planning** – it helps you to know when and how to keep in contact.

- Don't underestimate the value of **praise** when communicating with your business contacts.

- Most people respond **positively** to flattery.

Say it with feeling

What's important is the way you begin to build business relationships. In effect you're starting a process of persuasion. It's not easy, and often using words is just not enough. You have to be able to hook the other party into the idea that there is something in it for them. Once they accept this, you are more likely to get their attention.

Benefits are things that do something for people. One of the benefits of reading this book is helping you with your strategy for building brilliant business connections.

> **TIP**
>
> To be persuasive you should offer people reasons that reflect their point of view. You won't get far just by saying why you think they should do something.

Making your case understandable, by explaining complex issues in a way that is easy to comprehend, is a benefit. Always play to your own personal strengths. If you are a cool professional type, make sure you communicate in a factual and efficient way. If you want to sound friendly, more informal and approachable, make your characteristics match the message you wish to convey.

Touching emotions and intellect

It is said that people act on emotion, and justify with logic. To be an effective persuader you should not only offer good reasons for something but also create emotional goodwill at the same time.

If you need to persuade powerfully, bring in stories to connect with people's hearts as well as minds. If your objective is to motivate people to donate blood, you could tell a story about someone who needs blood for a serious operation. Successful fundraisers use emotive illustrations when persuading people to donate to charities and their appeals can bring in thousands of pounds in revenue.

Recommendations work wonders. If you have mutual connections, it is much easier to persuade when there are credible people to testify that your skills helped them in some way or other.

You should be able to come up with a number of people from your contacts whose name would add credibility and respect to yours. Do have the courtesy to check with them beforehand that you would like to mention their name to your new contact, as long as they have no objection. More often than not, there will be no problem. In fact they may even offer to contact them in advance to say you will be ringing.

Use several sources
If possible, don't rely on only one source for recommendations. Using several different parties gives further weight to your case. You increase your chances that one or other of your sources will be a powerful influence over the person with whom you're building up trust.

Don't waste their time

Ensuring that you are persuasive needs some
preparation. Think about how you want to come across
to your business contact. Ask yourself why anyone
should want to listen to you.

List your reasons and then organise them.

◆ What are the most important things you are trying to
  say.

◆ How can you build rapport with one another?

◆ Can you arrange your thoughts into a logical
  sequence? You could start with something attention-
  grabbing and continue to maintain interest
  throughout the exchange. Perhaps you want to build
  up your case throughout the dialogue and end with
  some weighty fact that has masses of impact.

Whatever you want to do, prepare for your encounter
with your business connection as if you were planning a
presentation. Make your content understandable and
attractive.

6

Keeping Up Appearances

Have something to say, and say it as clearly as you can. That is the only secret of style.

Matthew Arnold

We're now moving on to creating the right impression, building confidence and self-esteem. If these issues are something you are concerned about, these suggestions should help you create your winning strategy for building brilliant business connections.

FIRST IMPRESSIONS

Remember – you never have a second chance to make a first impression. Within a few moments, assumptions and judgements are made. You know it's true – we all do it. However hard you try to avoid doing so, you're likely to make an instant decision about someone because of the way they look, speak or what they wear.

Research says that when making an entrance:

◆ 55 per cent of the impression made is how you look – posture and what you wear
◆ 38 per cent is the energy and enthusiasm – body language and tone of voice

♦ only 7 per cent is what you actually say to a person.

Visual impressions, therefore, are more persuasive than oral messages.

If you get off to a good start, everything else you do afterwards will be just that much easier. A good beginning not only affects the business contact, it affects your confidence too. Confidence requires preparation and needs to be actively worked at to ensure you achieve the right impact.

When you are well prepared you will appear more confident, and better able to make a positive start to your important business relationship. This is not a question of tricks or gimmicks. It's about being businesslike and professional and aware of the importance of everything going well at the early stages. Having the intention is the first step towards achieving it.

LOOKING THE PART

Posture and body language

If you're serious about this and want to be like the professionals, ask your company to invest in some presentation training for you.

Some presentation trainers start by making a video of the way you walk, talk, stand and sit, and how you present yourself at meetings and corporate events. This is a fairly harsh way of finding out all your peccadilloes but it will help you to sort them out swiftly and effectively.

Even if you don't have the opportunity to get professional assistance, there is a lot you can do to help yourself.

Make a list of the areas you think need attention – such as weak posture and negative body language. Ask a close friend what they think you are good at, and what perhaps they think might be improved. Something even as simple as slouching at your desk is a bad habit. Many people have terrible posture and don't realise it.

One tip from the experts is to imagine 'a golden thread' running from the top of your head to the ceiling. When you stand or sit, imagine this thread is pulling you upright. You will grow taller and instantly be more noticeable.

Watch out for any indicators of nervousness or low self-confidence. These could be fidgeting, covering your mouth with your hand, tightly clasped hands, bowed head and avoiding eye contact.

It's a natural instinct when you're apprehensive to want to make yourself smaller. Crossing your arms or holding your bag in front of you are other give-aways.

Controlling your arms gives powerful clues as to how confident, open and receptive you are. Keeping your arms relaxed and to the side of your body shows you are not scared. You give the impression of being able to take whatever comes your way meeting things 'full frontal'.

The more outgoing you are, the more you'll use your arms to great effect with big movements and gestures. If you're the quiet type, you move your limbs less and keep them close to your body.

Looking self-assured

If you want to be seen as a confident and self-assured person, capable of conducting business negotiations in a cool professional manner, using open body language will make you more persuasive.

Stand upright, balanced on both feet with your weight evenly distributed. If you can pull in those abdominals you'll look not only taller but slimmer. Remember, your body is an instrument – it can convey every emotion.

Another tip is mirroring gestures. It's great for creating a good first impression with new business contacts. By copying what the other person does, it endorses the favourable view they've formed of you.

Actions speak louder than words and body language speaks volumes.

When you are trying to create a favourable impression with someone, your body will quite naturally point towards them – your face, hands, arms, feet and legs will be turned their way.

Make sure that you imitate the positive body language signs and not the negative ones. This reinforces the right impression and creates a bond between the parties.

These gestures can be quite subconscious, but they are picked up easily by the other person. You've probably noticed this dozens of times amongst people you've sat next to at work, when travelling or in social situations.

Try watching next time you've got a few moments to spare – observe how individuals position themselves when communicating with each other. You'll notice how they naturally angle themselves towards the person with whom they are trying to create a positive impression, and turn away from those they are seeking to avoid.

Eye contact

Making the correct sort of eye contact in business negotiations is important. Usually you are dealing with someone you don't know very well so there are a number of things to remember.

It is quite natural to look at people from eye to eye and across the top of the nose. This is the safe area to which eye contact should be confined. With friends, in social situations, this area of vision increases to include both eyes but also downwards to the nose and mouth. If you're flirting with someone, the scope of this triangle increases – widening at the base to involve more of the body.

As the object of the exercise is to do business with them rather than sleep with them, do pay attention if you find someone watching your mouth while you're talking to them. In body-language terms, they might be sending you a signal that they want to kiss you. I am not being gender specific here, so I think it's best to err on the side of caution!

If you're very nervous, try not to stare obsessively at someone when they are speaking to you. They could be forgiven for thinking that they've got something stuck to their chin, or that you are fixated on a particular facial feature. On the other hand, looking away completely, slow blinking or closing the eyes for longer periods than normal, can be a clear indication of lack of interest or, worse, boredom.

As a final point, remember that gestures can direct eye contact.

Pointing to something you are showing to your business contact directs his eyes towards it, lifting the head and engaging eye contact again will change the emphasis of your meeting. These hints may not be infallible, but they are useful and worth noting in the general context of relationship-building for business.

Getting a head start

If you want to stand out from your competitors and create the best impression for business purposes, use your head!

Keeping your head level both horizontally and vertically gives the impression of authority. A friendly gesture when listening to what your companion is saying is to tilt your head slightly to one side or the other.

Also remember that you were given two ears and only one mouth, so use them in that proportion. If you can spend twice as much time listening as talking, you will be creating a positive impression. People will regard you as a skilled communicator who knows how to initiate a conversation without dominating it.

CREATING IMPACT

Creating the right impact is essential. You can influence how you want your business contact to remember you by altering the first impression. Each situation requires a slightly different focus. You would behave more informally at a party than if you were meeting at a corporate event or in the boardroom.

Your dress should show authority and inspire confidence, but don't forget you need to express approachability, too. Be clear about the image you want to create. Don't be fussy – aim to be remembered positively.

Avoid fashion gaffes. Clothes matter and it's far safer to be well groomed, stylishly dressed and somewhat conservative.

Following high fashion trends is not appropriate in a corporate setting – unless, of course, you are in the fashion industry. Being a *Sex in the City* look-alike may be desirable in some circumstances but it's not universally appropriate. Designer labels are a luxury for many, and are not essential.

Your meeting is the first of what you hope will be a mutually rewarding business relationship, so it's important to choose an outfit that fits well and is comfortable. It should be attractive, flattering and, above all, appropriate to the occasion. Don't try going for a radical change of image – it's too risky. Leave the hot pants and gold lamé at home for another occasion.

> **KEY POINT**
>
> It's far more important to have well manicured hands, clean well cut hair and good quality accessories. If the overall impression given is that you are well groomed, then you're winning.

Clothes that are tight are a nightmare. Not only are they unflattering, they create completely the wrong impression. You'll probably be a bit apprehensive anyway, so tightly fitting clothes will mean you can't breathe or move freely. You'll feel uncomfortable if you eat or drink anything while you're in the meeting and the last thing you need is any possible embarrassment – such as a button flying off or a zip bursting open.

Don't forget your feet. If possible, don't wear new shoes to important business functions. You should avoid shoes that pinch or that have three-inch heels. If you can't stand or walk comfortably in them, find another pair. Be less ambitious and play safe.

Who knows, you might be asked to accompany your business contact on an inspection of the whole of their new office headquarters, or be kept standing for ages while waiting to meet someone at a reception line-up. You want to be able to glide like a swan, not waddle around like a duck with gout!

BE OUTSTANDING

One of the easiest ways to outshine everyone and appear charming is to smile. Many people have the most wonderful natural smiles, but due to nervousness or apprehension, all that seems to be registering on their faces are the stress muscles.

A smile lights up a face – so use yours to good effect. People who smile give the impression of being pleasant, attractive, sincere and confident. It relaxes those with whom you are making contact.

Good manners never go amiss and that applies both to you and to your business contact. Always use your charm and remember to say thank you.

If you have an appointment, be punctual. On a first meeting the overriding impression should be that you are capable of arriving somewhere on time. If you turn up late, whatever the reason, all that your contact will remember is that you missed the appointment. It could mean that this first encounter will be your last.

However organised you are, to avoid stress allow yourself extra time if you are travelling. If you arrive for your meeting in a fluster and out of breath, you'll be in the wrong frame of mind to get the most out of the occasion. Appearing cool, calm and collected is well worth the extra investment of a taxi ride if that's all it takes.

PAY ATTENTION

This may sound like unnecessary advice, but it is surprising how many people can't stop their eyes straying when someone walks past an office or a commotion takes place outside. Keep your eyes and ears directed towards the other person at all times. If you can create the impression that they have all your attention, you will have made excellent progress towards building a positive working relationship.

Always switch off your mobile phone. There's no better way to kill off goodwill at a business meeting than being interrupted by an unwanted bleeping coming from your pocket or bag. Don't compound the sin by answering your phone.

This applies the other way round too. If your business contact has the insensitivity to receive calls and messages throughout your meeting, it's an insult. It shows a lack of respect for you and creates completely the wrong impression.

There are occasions when such interruptions are unavoidable. But if you are conducting a meeting while expecting an important call, have the courtesy to say so. If the phone call does interrupt your dialogue, explain politely that it is the call you'd been expecting, and could they excuse you for a moment while you respond. Make a discreet exit and be brief!

Don't forget the props. You are trying to look efficient.

This can be influenced by things beyond clothes and grooming. You may look fine until you open your briefcase – if what's inside looks like the contents of the average rubbish dump, it's not going to work in your favour.

You also need to be prepared for the occasion. If you are going to attend a site meeting with an architect or a quantity surveyor, you may need a pair of boots and a hard hat. Perhaps you are likely to be inspecting machinery, in which case you may need some protective clothing. Make sure that you take them with you or that they are in the back of your car, ready to hand in case you need them.

MORALE BOOSTING

You should have a plan for boosting your morale. With greater self-esteem you will have the confidence required to conduct business negotiations in the most favourable and positive way.

APPEARANCES SUMMARY

To recap – consider a little self-analysis. Get some feedback from others on how they see you. Ask yourself and a few trusted friends these questions:

◆ What are the situations and occasions where you most lack confidence? Create a list and see if there are any recurring themes and triggers.

◆ What kind of image do you currently project?

◆ What impression do you make on people at a first meeting?

◆ How do existing contacts react towards you?

♦ What one behavioural trait might be worth
  changing?

Consider the information you get. Try to concentrate on
a positive mental attitude. Build yourself up so that you
start to believe in your own ability to succeed. Behave
and look as if you have already achieved your goals.
Confidence breeds confidence and as it develops, it will
become natural to you and have a positive impact on
others.

It doesn't matter who you are, people will make
judgements based on their first impressions. One of the
key reasons why you need to spend time and effort on
your appearance is to give yourself that confidence
boost so that you feel self-assured. Once you've achieved
this, there'll be no holding you back.

Remember the four main areas:

♦ posture
♦ clothing – flattering and appropriate
♦ overall impression – well groomed, professional,
  understated
♦ manners and use of your own unique strengths.

The outcome of many situations is often determined by
the confidence shown by the parties involved. A lack of
skill or knowledge can go unnoticed. A conflict can be
resolved or a business contract won purely through a

display of confidence.

Self-belief and self-assurance are vital if you are to realise your potential and maximise your success through brilliant business connections. By challenging your thinking and working on the areas that need adapting, you can make a positive start. Confidence is like a muscle – it needs to be worked to be developed.

7

The Art of Communicating

You impress folks that little bit more with what
you're saying if you say it nicely. People don't
hear your ideas if you just stand there shouting
out the words.

Lord Gormley

You've reached the point at which you're about to have
that first meeting with your brilliant business contact.
It's a milestone in the relationship-building process and
your communications skills will be tested to the limit.

Face-to-face meetings can result in awkward pauses and
initial shyness for those who are not brimming with
confidence. To help you over this hurdle, you can
approach the meeting fully prepared and well armed if
you have a look at the following factors.

In order to get your message across, think about what
you are trying to achieve during the dialogue:

♦ What information do you wish to convey?
♦ What do you want the other person to do as a result?

Organise yourself beforehand. Jot down notes about your major points. Be positive and keep the message simple.

CLARITY IS PARAMOUNT

What is communication? In short, it's signalling. The transmission, by speaking, writing or gestures, of information which evokes understanding.

That's simple enough, isn't it? Straightforward in theory but in practice it's fraught with dangers – particularly if you have high expectations from these important business connections.

Communication is not just speaking, writing or gesticulating. It's more than the transmission of information. Something else has to occur for the communication to be complete. The other party in the communication process has to engage their brain and receive the message.

When dealing with business relationships, it's quite complex. There are plenty of opportunities for misunderstanding and miscommunication.

The previous chapter dealt with the importance of making a good first impression – how appearance and body language can make or break the initial few seconds of an initial encounter, but what happens when you open your mouth?

If you manage to insert both feet with speed and agility, you will undo in an instant all the hard work that went before! If you're nervous, don't be surprised if words come out which you seemingly have no ability to control. A conversation can go seriously wrong before you've had time to sit down.

There are some points to remember when considering the various methods of communication and some hazards to be aware of when dealing with business relationships:

- Only 7% of the impact you make comes from the words you speak.

- The rest is visual – your appearance, the sound of your voice and your body language.

- You can break that 7% further down into sections:
  - the type of words you use
  - the sort of sentences you use
  - how you phrase them.

If you want to make a favourable impression on your business contact, consider the words, ideas and structure of the message you wish to convey. Keep it simple if you possibly can. Always aim for clarity over ambiguity.

- Commonly-used words, in short direct sentences, have the greatest impact and allow the least margin for error or misinterpretation.

- Long words wrapped in complex sentences are confusing and best avoided. Don't use jargon either.

- Positive statements are far more acceptable and will gain you greater advantage than negatively expressed remarks.

VOICING YOUR THOUGHTS

Pay attention to your voice. Tone, inflection, volume and pitch are all areas to consider. Most people don't need to develop their speaking voice, but there are many who do not understand how to use it effectively.

The simplest way is to compare the voice to a piece of music – it is the voice that is the instrument of interpretation of the spoken word.

Those who have had some training in public speaking sometimes use mnemonics as memory joggers for optimum vocal effect. One simple example is R S V P P P:

- Rhythm
- Speed
- Voice
- Pitch
- Pause
- Projection.

Rhythm
Speaking without variety of tone can anaesthetise your listener. Try raising and lowering the voice to bring

vocal sound to life and keep your audience awake! Rhythm is directly linked with speed.

Speed

Speed variation is connected to the vocal rhythm. Varying speed makes for interested listeners and helps them maintain concentration. If you're recounting a story, speed helps to add excitement to the tale, but the speed of delivery should be matched with the volume you're speaking at.

Volume

The level of volume obviously depends on where the conversation is taking place. It would be inappropriate to be loud when speaking in a one-to-one situation. However, you'd probably need to increase it if you were talking in a crowded venue, such as a business reception or work area. Volume is used mainly for emphasis and to command attention – lowering your voice can add authority when telling an interesting story or giving advice.

Pitch

Pitching your voice is something public speakers do. They are trained to 'throw' their voices so they can deliver their speech clearly to their audience in whatever size or shape of room they're speaking in. In general, it's irritating to any listener if they have to strain to hear what the speaker is saying.

In normal conversations where you need to be heard clearly (for example, in restaurants where there is continual background noise as well as the hubbub of other voices), it's impossible to pitch your voice if you hardly open your mouth to let the words out. Correct use of mouth, jaw and lip muscles will produce properly accentuated words and assist with clear enunciation. Pay attention to these facial muscles otherwise your voice will be just a dull monotone.

Pause

Practise the pause. It can be the most effective use of your voice though it is often ignored. A pause should last about four seconds. It sounds like an eternity perhaps but anything shorter will go unnoticed by your listener. You can use the time to maintain good eye contact. The effect can be dynamite.

Remember the 'er' count. Filling spaces in conversation with props such as 'ers', 'ums' or 'you knows' where there should be pauses are clear signs of nervousness and should be avoided.

Projection

This encompasses everything about the way you come across: power, personality, weight, authority, and expertise – what some people call 'clout'. You want to build some long-lasting powerful business connections, so it pays to have some 'gravitas' in your dealings with people. Projection is an art which can be practised, but you can learn so much from listening to experienced communicators – they have it in spades!

REVIEWING YOUR VOCAL SKILLS

If possible, get a colleague or a friend to give you feedback on your voice and mannerisms. Unless you get an accurate appraisal, you could be spoiling your chances of successful business exchanges. With practice you'll be surprised how quickly some of these traits can be eradicated. Once you've eliminated them and developed some of the skills suggested here, the improvement in your style of conversation and self-confidence when meeting people will be remarkable.

Remember, your voice is an instrument – just like your body. It is also, like your body, very flexible. You know the expression 'It's not what you say, it's the way that you say it'? That couldn't be more true.

◆ Be clear – use simple, easily understood words and phrases.

◆ Be loud enough for your listener to hear you.

◆ Be assertive – a bright and confident tone will inject interest into anything you're saying.

◆ Do stop for breath – it's essential to let your listener digest what you've said – and to have the opportunity to respond!

To help you build your brilliant business connections you need polished communication skills. If you can harness these to your other attributes, you will be well on the way to making these relationships rewarding and profitable.

FACE-TO-FACE ENCOUNTERS

The key to success is to get onto your business contact's wavelength as soon as possible. By putting yourself in his shoes you'll demonstrate your ability to empathise with him. He'll find communicating with you easy and will show positive responses.

One of the most important aspects of communicating is to develop good listening skills. By listening you will pick up quickly on the areas of common ground between you.

KEY POINT

Many people are not good listeners. You are not alone if you are far more interested in what you have to say, or what the people standing next to you at the business reception are saying. Poor listening damages exchanges and that is what you are at pains to avoid.

Good listening avoids misunderstandings and the errors that result from them. The behaviour of a good listener is as follows:

♦ A person who is listening attentively keeps a comfortable level of eye contact and has an open and relaxed but alert pose. You should face the speaker and respond to what he is saying with appropriate facial expressions, offering encouragement with a nod or a smile.

◆ Adopting the behaviour of a good listener will help you establish good rapport with your business contact. It requires a degree of self-discipline and a genuine desire to take on board the message the speaker is trying to convey. You need to be able to suspend judgement and avoid contradicting or interrupting him. Postpone saying your bit until you are sure he has finished and you have understood his point.

◆ Reflecting and summarising – repeating back a key word or phrase the speaker has used – shows you have listened and understood. Summarising gives the speaker a chance to add to or amend your understanding. Your business contact is far more likely to listen to you if you have let him know that you have heard what he said by using the tactics of reflecting and summarising.

You should avoid:

◆ thinking up clever counter-arguments before he has finished making his point

◆ interrupting unnecessarily or reacting emotionally to anything that is said

◆ if the subject becomes dull or complex, registering

your disinterest by succumbing to distractions or fidgeting.

THE FIVE LEVELS OF LISTENING SKILLS

There are five levels of listening skills and it pays to remember them.

The first and worst level is **ignoring the speaker**. You look away, avoid eye contact and do something else altogether. (I get this sort of reaction from my family much of the time! The lights are on but nobody's there.) This is dreadful in a business context. Your hard-earned business contact will never give you the time of day again if you commit this cardinal sin.

The second level, which is almost as bad, is to **pretend to listen**. In some ways this can be quite dangerous. If you're nodding your head, and saying 'mmm, yes, aha' when you actually have no idea what's being said, you could be in for a nasty shock. Don't be surprised if you hear your business contact saying, 'So you'll run in the London Marathon next year on behalf of my favourite charity – how wonderful!' – you deserved that!

The third-level listening skill is being **selective**. You may well find yourself listening for key words that are of importance, such as 'business opportunities', 'budgets' or 'new suppliers'. The result is that you'll miss the main content of the exchange. Your contact could have been telling you that there are no openings for business until the end of the next financial year.

If you can develop the fourth-level skill, you're doing well. This is called **being attentive**. You are focused, with positive body language, leaning forward, nodding your head appropriately and maintaining eye contact. Your business contact knows you're paying attention and this creates an atmosphere where he'll want to share valuable information and engage in serious dialogue.

The final level is **being empathetic**. Empathy is the ability to put yourself in someone else's place and see things from their perspective. This takes time to achieve but it will knock the socks off anyone once you have reached it. It is the art of being able to identify mentally and emotionally with your communicator, fully comprehending the tones, pitch, body language and other subtle messages your contact is conveying.

It is totally exhausting to do this for any length of time but it will take your business relationship to a much higher level rapidly. You will have included each other in the closest of possible personal networks (sometimes called a virtual team). He will consider you one of his first ports of call when information gathering or project awarding is required, and you'll willingly reciprocate.

DIRECTING THE COMMUNICATION CYCLE

Can you recall a time when you've been chatting to a work colleague, or a friend, and you've looked at your watch and said 'Wow, is that the time? I must have been talking to you for ages.'? This usually happens when the two people concerned are giving each other space in their conversation. There is a feeling of ease, ideas are being passed to and fro, and a natural exchange develops. It's a bit like having a conversational game of table tennis. This is called rapport.

If you can begin to build rapport with your business connections you will be making great progress in establishing the relationship you want and your exchanges will become frequent and more valuable. You're attempting to establish the balance of listening and talking.

There are times when you'll want to find out more information. It's easy to ask too many questions and fall into a sort of 'Spanish Inquisition' situation. Conversely when responding to a question you can give away too much information. If you're on the receiving end of this from your business contact, the relationship may not make much progress. No one likes to feel they are being 'pumped' for information. It's infuriating and insulting and you'll want to distance yourself as quickly as possible.

IDENTIFYING A COMMON LANGUAGE

Only one person at a time can truly direct a conversation. One leads and the other tends to follow. This doesn't mean there is no give and take. Neither does it mean that the other party is subservient. But one of the parties should lead and there is merit in you being the one that does so. Your objective after all is to build a proactive business relationship with rewards for both sides.

Opening rituals

At the start of a meeting, there are usually some general opening remarks, possibly about the weather or the state of the traffic or where to park. This sort of opening ritual is customary and should take no longer than a few minutes at the outset of proceedings. Watch for the moment when the chattiness should cease because if you have no real plan, your contact may lead you off into uncharted waters and you'll find yourself heading in the wrong direction.

Someone usually starts off by saying, 'Right, shall we move on? Can you tell me...' That person should be you. If you don't seize the opportunity to take control at this point in your exchange, you may have lost the initiative for the rest of the meeting.

You might consider going into the meeting with a short agenda. If this isn't written down, it should at least be in your head. It could be little more than a few helpful suggestions. Perhaps you've already aired the topics for discussion in a telephone call beforehand. There is no rule here, but whatever has been agreed it does at least mean that the exchange proceeds along some agreed lines.

It also provides an element of control during the

dialogue if the conversation meanders into other areas. You could refer back to your brief by saying something like, 'we were going to discuss X next ...' and then move on smoothly to the next stage.

The early part of any meeting is a key stage for your confidence; you'll feel and operate better if you get off to a planned start and you'll be able to maintain better control and direct the rest of the exchange.

GOOD CONVERSATIONAL TECHNIQUES

To develop a balanced style of communication, try to begin the conversation by introducing yourself and giving some personal information. This is called the **inform** stage.

Once you've given some information, ask a direct question of your business contact. This is called the **invite** stage.

Then **wait** for his response.

On receiving this, **listen** to every word!

Then **acknowledge** and, if necessary, repeat the essence of their response.

If you achieve this cycle of communication you can repeat it many times over during the encounter to establish a good rapport between you both. It should make the time pass effortlessly and harmoniously and make your business relationship a pleasant experience.

Business relationship-building has similarities to the dating process. You are attempting to get closer to your prospect by developing the art of good conversation, so pay attention to the importance of **eye contact**. This has been covered in the previous chapter, but it is so important it is worth recapping here.

Appropriate eye contact at all times in the business exchange is essential. If, while you are talking, you notice that your contact is looking at you with an interested expression, nodding occasionally and smiling at the right times with an alert and open posture, you're holding his attention and doing everything right.

THINGS TO LOOK OUT FOR

Should your business contact appear to be falling asleep during one of your conversational gambits, it could mean that:

- he's had a late night
- he's had an early start
- he's suffering from jet lag
- the atmosphere in the room is too stuffy
- your dialogue is rather boring.

Don't wait until his head falls forward and hits the

desk. If you fail to notice until you hear the crash, you're definitely talking too much!

Keep an eye out too for fidgeting, this could indicate that:

- you've lost his attention
- he wants a break
- he's irritated by something you've said
- he finds the conversation irrelevant.

Whatever the reason, it's time to shut up. Close your mouth without delay and smile. Hopefully with a bit of silence you can retrieve a relationship that may have got off to a rather inauspicious start.

When your business contact starts shaking his head, this could mean:

- he wants to say something
- he doesn't agree with you
- he simply hasn't a clue what you're waffling on about.

Again, it's time to bring your remarks to a swift close.

If you think you've lost his attention completely and he's turned off, try to regain it by asking him a pertinent question. Re-establish eye contact and vary the volume or expression in your voice.

OTHER FORMS OF ORAL COMMUNICATION

Telephone calls

These can be difficult to deal with and can often cause trouble between parties who do not know each other all that well.

First, because you can't see each other face-to-face, you have to rely on tone of voice. This can be deceptive. He may sound uninterested because he's talking in a low voice. It may be something as simple as the fact that he's got a sore throat, or he's trying to avoid the rest of the office hearing his conversation.

It's essential to pay attention when your new business contact calls. If he's on a mobile, you may well get a distortion due to background noise, traffic, airport announcements or similar. If possible take the phone call in a private place so as to avoid even more noise coming from your end of the phone.

Voicemail messages

There's an art to leaving successful voicemail messages. It's simply this: be clear and be concise.

Don't speak too fast. If you are leaving your telephone number, slow down. Speak slowly while recording the information.

> I remember spending a number of weeks in increasing frustration some time ago trying to reach a potentially important business contact who'd rung and left me a message. He'd spoken so quickly I could not transcribe the number. I dialled whatever number I thought he'd said, but never reached him. When he rang me again – after numerous unsuccessful attempts at reaching him – I explained that I'd tried to return his call but had given up. I had been getting through to the Accounts Department at Selfridges. He works at one of the large city law firms and thought it was rather funny!

If the message you leave is either gabbled or garbled, it will be impossible for any one to return your call. It helps to leave a date and time when you record your message, so that your contact can respond quickly if time is critical.

WRITTEN COMMUNICATION

The main point about written communication is that whatever form it takes, the recipient cannot see you or hear you. Your contact has no option but to accept what they read. You should pay particular attention to wording and expressions because if it is at all ambiguous, it is liable to be misinterpreted.

Letters

When handwriting letters put yourself in the position of your recipient. Write neatly and clearly and make sure your spelling is correct. It helps to use a decent pen and good quality paper. Impressions count, remember!

With a personal thank you note, use your contact's business address because it is after all a business relationship, even though you are thanking him for inviting you to a social occasion. Keep your message simple and make it easy to read. Layout is important. Avoid innuendo, sarcasm and *doubles entendres.*

Electronic mail

Much has been written about email etiquette because this is such a popular and efficient form of communication.

If you wish to email to your business contact, check which address is the most appropriate. There may be confidentiality issues – particularly if your exchanges have something to do with career progression – and a personal email address may be more appropriate.

If he says it's okay to email to his business address, do be circumspect. Emails may not always reach the recipient directly. Some people have staff who scan emails before forwarding on to the main addressee. Consider the likelihood that your email is going to be read by someone else, so be extra careful. Any references to personal habits (his, yours or other people's) can be so rapidly transmitted around the world by an enthusiastic prankster.

On a more practical level, email is not the medium for rambling on and on about a project dear to your heart. Keep email communication clear and short. It's no substitute for face-to-face contact, but it does allow for a fast exchange of information, particularly when confirming meetings or referring to matters just discussed.

Text messages

This is the perfect form of communication for quick exchanges of information.

One word of warning on this one – don't use confusing abbreviations. A colleague of mine received the following message – CU 7.30. Did that mean 'See you at 7.30pm' or 'Curtain Up at 7.30pm'? She interpreted it as the former and missed the play!

COMMUNICATION SKILLS AWARENESS CHECKLIST

Presence – Pay attention to the way your voice and body language are used in conjunction with the words you speak. You can convey the right impression if they are used correctly.

Relating – Don't underestimate the importance of developing your rapport-building skills to get on the same wavelength as your business prospect.

Questioning – When engaged in conversation with your contact, make sure you match your question to the situation or subject. Beware asking irrelevant questions – this will show that you've not paid attention to what he has said.

Listening – Listen to everything he says attentively. Try to reach at least Level Four. If he's likely to become a significant influence in your business development strategy you should aim for achieving Level Five eventually.

Checking – The art of glancing at your business contact to see that he's still on your wavelength while you're engaged in dialogue. Watch for gestures and see whether he does the same when he's talking to you.

8

How Far Can This Relationship-Building Process Go?

> Be nice to people on your way up because you'll meet 'em on your way down.
>
> *Wilson Mizner*

MAKE YOUR CORPORATE CONNECTIONS WORK FOR YOU

This is the next important stage. You've created the database, sorted through your contacts and categorised them. You've also spent some time working out the links and connections that already exist.

You've reviewed your own personal strengths and characteristics and have checked on your appearance and your communication skills.

Now you need to think what types of people you will be dealing with. Who is included in your collection of business contacts? If you can identify them easily, you won't waste precious time and resources dealing with them in the wrong way.

By paying attention to detail you will find that when you contact someone they will most likely be pleased to see or hear from you. This will make the process of building brilliant connections easier and more successful.

> **KEY POINT**
>
> Study human behaviour. Every business solution comes down to influencing people. *Sir John Collins, Chairman of Dixons Group, Ex-Chairman of National Power*

Be proactive with your connections. You've created a network that is vibrant and dynamic, unique to you and your business. You don't want to be hit and miss. A thoroughly joined-up network is the most powerful asset. If you make sure it is part of your business development strategy, it will work wonders for you and your company.

It's perhaps easier if you look inside your organisation first. No doubt in your database you have entered your colleagues, staff, team members and superiors. You could usefully spend a bit of time working out what makes them 'tick'. Once you get into the habit of doing this when you meet people, it is amazing how easily and successfully you can connect.

Have you changed your car recently? Before you got the new make or model, were you aware how many of them existed? I expect you hardly ever noticed them. But once you'd taken delivery of yours, isn't it amazing how many other similar models you find as you drive around? Suddenly there are lots of them all over the place.

This also applies to people. Once you've identified a particular type, you will find that you meet other people who remind you of them. Whether they are physically similar, temperamentally alike or just have the same attributes, you will probably know instinctively how they'll react, what they will be like when you speak to them and how to get on their wavelength.

INTERNAL RELATIONSHIP-BUILDING IN THE WORKPLACE

Companies prosper when staff are genuinely interested in their colleagues and others.

This requires mutual respect and, in some cases, developing the confidence to build appropriate relationships within the workplace. (See Chapter 6 for information on confidence building.)

Impressions do count – particularly at work.

◆ How do staff members come across to one another in your organisation?

◆ Do your staff interact easily and with openness?

◆ Any anxieties or insecurities will hinder good communication. Those who feel threatened or undervalued will have the greatest difficulty in buying into the culture of rapport-building, or feeling motivated about their work.

If your perceptions are at variance with happier colleagues, you will find it difficult to adapt to change. You may feel threatened because any movement away from the 'old order' will be seen as yet another unwelcome alteration. If you don't go with the flow, you will be less at ease and feel alienated.

People tend to be one of two types – extrovert or introvert, or those who are people-oriented and those who are highly task-aware.

The latter type often find it difficult to appreciate the value of personal contacts. You may have a colleague like this. They would rather sit at their desk, staring at the computer screen. They email people they sit next to rather than speak to them! They certainly avoid getting coffee from the machine so they don't have to strike up conversations with colleagues.

People like this do exist – I've worked with some of them and it's staggering what they'll do to avoid contact with colleagues. Sometimes they try to cover it up by saying they haven't got time to chat and there's too much gossip anyway.

A bit of staff bonding goes a long way to enhance goodwill amongst team members and colleagues.

- How much do staff members really know about each other?

- Who are the key people within your organisation to network with?

- Which ones are the decision-makers, the movers and shakers, the influential persuaders?

- Are there some well-connected people – your former bosses or colleagues who have now moved on?

You may not think about this much, but your colleagues and your boss are just other human beings. They have hopes, fears and insecurities like you. Sometimes they need nurturing.

Try to cultivate the ability to see the world from other people's perspectives. Find out how your colleagues or boss prefer to work. Then, fit in with the pattern so that you can become a fully inclusive member of the team.

Watch out for the stress points. Don't make a lot of noise early in the morning if some of your colleagues prefer to start the day quietly. If your antennae are tuned in, you will be able to pick up on the clues – when interruptions are welcome and when not – and make sure you don't add to the distractions.

Whether you are building business relationships internally or externally, it pays to spend time finding out people's likes and dislikes.

A 'thank you' never comes amiss. If praise is due, then say something. If it can be done appropriately, in public, the results can be dynamic.

OUTWARD LOOKING

You are looking at ways of building rapport. Start within your organisation, and practise your skills here before working on your wider network. It is useful to consider the 'O' words in this connection.

- Seek **opportunities** to make connections with colleagues on every **occasion**. Where? Anywhere you happen to be.

- Within your **organisation**, have a look at the management structure, research information about the company and look around you.

- What are the **objectives** you want to achieve while working there?

- How do you go about trying to be **outstanding**?

- If you are intent on enhancing your career prospects, be **overt**.

- What do you do to make yourself **obvious** – in a positive light?

- As mentioned earlier, presentation counts. In order to make connections, **offer** people something.

- Always keep an eye out for **openings**, whether this is to introduce yourself to new people or get involved with new projects or incentives.

- An **ongoing** effort will be required and as you gain in confidence, coincidences will **occur**. The possibilities are endless once you have started to look up from your desk and extend your horizons.

- The more adept you become at making friends and winning people over, the easier you will find it when trying to **overcome obstacles** that may hold you up.

Who is who? Inside your company, which people do you need to influence? Who do you know well enough to ask for support when you need it? In other words, who is in your inner circle?

CREATING A STAKEHOLDER MAP

Creating a stakeholder map is a useful exercise for anyone within a large organisation who needs to know the right people. Consider the following:

- Who do you need to get to know better?

- How often do you currently make contact with them?

- What opportunities exist, or do you need to create, to connect with them, either in or out of the office?

- Do you have an identified 'hot list' of contacts? These are your 'inner circle' who can help you and influence others at times when support is needed – say when promotion or job opportunities occur.

My inner circle consists of perhaps ten people. They are people I know extremely well and for whom I have huge amounts of respect. Sometimes I get 'stuck' on a problem or issue. By telephoning one or two of them and asking, 'what would you do?', 'have you ever come up against this?' or 'who would you talk to?', I get a quick injection of common sense, or a radical solution to what I had thought was an insuperable problem.

They may be people within your organisation, or come from another aspect of your life – from school days, wider family members, former colleagues or friends. The whole point about your virtual team is that you would be prepared to do for them what they are prepared to do for you:

KEY POINT

You will find there are probably no more than about six to ten people who will be in your close circle of trusted allies. This 'virtual team' is an essential aid to building brilliant business connections.

- ◆ You're sincerely interested in them and what they are doing.

- ◆ You know their likes and dislikes and are genuinely interested in their success and happiness.

- ◆ Whatever it takes, you keep in regular contact.

- ◆ You're alert to opportunities for introducing them to new people.

- ◆ You send regular informative emails or meet up for a coffee and chat.

You're wise enough not to go to them just with your problems. You keep your visibility high, always maintaining them in the loop as to what you are doing, and making them aware of new developments in your career, business or profession as appropriate.

You'd stick up for them, write a glowing reference, support them, listen sympathetically to their concerns, spring into action for them – whatever it takes. You would trust them with your life and they would do the same for you!

IDENTIFYING KEY PLAYERS

Influential people

These are not necessarily people in high places. If you have a wide range of contacts, you will find that some people who are not in powerful positions of seniority can wield considerable power. Let me offer two examples.

This is extracted from *Making Management Simple (Change Management)* published by How To Books

The board of a company decided as part of their modernisation that they needed to join two buildings together which were separated by a busy road. They commissioned architects and consultants to apply to the local planning department to build a bridge between the two factories. The application was refused. They spent many hours and much money researching other solutions but came up with none. The board and the consultants were stuck.

One morning the chairman of the board was driving to work and saw ahead of him the caretaker on the other side of the road. The man disappeared into the building but by the time the chairman passed that spot he saw to his amazement the caretaker standing on the other side of the road. The chairman stopped his car and shouted to the caretaker, 'How did you do that? Get from one side of the road to the other without walking across?'

Answer? There was an underground maintenance passage. For some reason it was not on the building sites plans but it was in daily use by a small section of the workforce.

Moral: never be too proud to ask, nor underestimate the knowledge and experience of every single person you work with.

Another example:
Andrew, a friend of mine, used to work for a large international company which was hierarchical in its approach. One day he needed the advice of the chairman on a particular matter. He went through the usual channels and asked the chairman's PA if he could possibly see him for ten minutes. She replied that he was not available for two weeks.

> Andrew knew the decision could not wait, so he went
> to find the chairman's chauffeur. He asked Charles
> (the chauffeur) if he knew where the chairman was.
> Charles told him to be at the main entrance at 3.00pm
> that day as he was driving the chairman to the airport.
> Andrew was waiting by the door, as suggested, at the
> appointed time. The chairman spoke to him, and
> invited him to ride with him to the airport. The advice
> was given and the problem was solved.

So small talk can make a big difference:

- Be prepared to think laterally to solve problems.

- Remember a small piece of information can make a huge amount of difference.

- Powerful personal connections doesn't mean getting to know just 'the great and the good'.

- Pay attention to everyone and discover their individual strengths.

- Sometimes a valuable piece of information can come from the most unlikely source.

Movers and shakers
They usually far exceed the boundaries of their office positions. They make it their business to see and be seen. Identify them among your contacts, as they are important to keep track of – you never know where they are going to turn up next.

Corporate citizens

These are the hardworking, non-political types, who are great resources for information and advice.

They usually know the inside and outside of their business, their department and most personnel. If you nurture them and seek their advice when appropriate, they will be flattered. Better to ask them than find them saying afterwards, 'If only you'd asked me, I could have told you that.'

Keep an eye out for fire-fighters, vetoers and whiners. They are best avoided!

TYPES OF PEOPLE

Some people you know may be highly task-aware, while others are more people-oriented. You will build your most valuable connections with people who like dealing with other people.

Roadrunners

They are usually highly task-aware and will not let anyone stand in their way to achieve targets. They can be quite dangerous and it is wise to let them pass if you find you are in their way. Otherwise you could be roughly elbowed aside or, worse still, flattened as they rush past.

Racehorses

They get things done fast but like to ask others to help

them – they're very good at team work. A race-horse is
a valuable asset in any group. They are strong and
capable and can achieve great things. Harness them to
the right group and you will have a winning
combination.

New pups
You must know some of these. They are the most
people-oriented types and prefer to be with others
rather than alone. However they often have fairly low
awareness of the importance of getting things done and
are not the best at keeping to deadlines. Charming,
friendly and extremely social though they may be, you
need to be aware of their weaknesses – such as not
finishing work on time.

Tomcats
They prefer to be left alone to get on with their work.
They are independent, and are unaware of other people
and the importance of teams. Some of them are boffins
(lonely geniuses) and produce amazing results. They are
often in a world of their own and happiest in their own
company.

PERSUASION TECHNIQUES

Some people use a bit of psychology when dealing with
others. One theory is that people have different energies
and are therefore represented by a colour. There are
four main types:

Cool blue. They are usually regarded as the aloof types. They can be cautious, precise, deliberate and formal. You will find they are a bit distant and hold off getting close to people. If you are trying to work with them, or influence them, you will need to plan carefully and work on them slowly.

Fiery red. These people are pretty much the opposite of the blues. They are competitive, demanding, determined and strong willed. They will reach their goals whatever it takes, even if they have to knock you out of the way in order to do so, like road runners. If you are one of these, you might have to tone down your actions if you want to get ahead with the help of other people.

Sunshine yellow. Yellows are sociable, dynamic, demonstrative, enthusiastic and persuasive. What lovely people they are – an asset to any organisation or group. They have natural charisma and are able to shine in any situation. People naturally gravitate towards them and they are at ease in most situations. They're valued members of the team and they help keep morale high amongst colleagues. No matter how difficult the job is, they try to see things in a positive light.

Earth green. These are the caring, sharing, encouraging, compassionate and patient individuals. You probably know a number of them. They are kind and helpful and just can't help it! If you've got a green tinge, you're the

---

> **TIP**
>
> If you want to get on with people who are not like you, you could try adopting the chameleon approach – change colours to suit the environment you're in.

one in the office who always has the headache tablets, doesn't forget to water the plants and remembers colleagues' children's birthdays, even when they forget!

CONNECTION POINTS

How do you best communicate with people? Depending on who you want to contact, how well you know them, and what the desired outcome is, choose your method wisely.

Verbal

The most common way of communicating with people is by the written word.

Following a meeting with a potentially exciting business contact, if you are able to launch into print easily, a persuasive letter or a politely worded email will ensure that you are remembered. It emphasises that you are trustworthy and that you are organised and professional.

Continuous communication over a period of time establishes the connection. It builds trust.

The power of thank you is tremendous. Send thank you notes after each event you attend, or when someone does something for you. It means, 'We value your business and appreciate the manner in which you conduct it.' A handwritten note is best. It's far ahead of the phone because the recipient knows it takes more effort. People appreciate thoughtfulness and don't forget kindness.

Oral

The art of conversation, or idle gossip? The chapter on communicating dealt with the 'dos and don'ts' of oral exchanges. In some work situations, where the Protestant version of the work ethic prevails, the belief is that to chatter is idle. 'Shooting the breeze' doesn't get the job done.

If you compare this to the continental approach, I think I prefer the European way. The first hour in French, Spanish and Italian offices is spent kissing! The second is where you exchange the latest gossip and the third is taken up going out for coffee and a croissant. OK, so I exaggerate!

Being gossip-averse can be short-sighted. Conversation is the way relationships are formed. Perhaps I should define 'gossip' as being useful chat rather than spreading malicious rumours about someone's reputation or latest conquest.

Relationships between people are a company's greatest asset. If people can't work together you won't have a successful business. Employees who can hold good-quality conversations with each other are valuable to any organisation.

Conversation should not be confused with communication. Communication is about exchanging information. Conversation is a creative process and engages people's minds.

Conversations don't stick to agendas, neither do they incorporate jargon or management theory and hype. Conversations are about connectivity – enabling staff to keep in touch with one another. They are an antidote to stress and other health problems. People who have good social relationships at work are far less likely to be anxious, stressed, absent or seeking to move on.

TIP

It's good to talk! Gossip and conversation encourage business too. So don't just have a solitary coffee and read your emails, go and ask a colleague to take a break and sit and chat together for a few minutes.

Using your intuition

If you are having difficulty connecting with someone, step back for a moment and reflect. Sit and think about the way you felt about that person when you first met them.

◆ What initial reactions did you get?
◆ Were you impressed with their voice?
◆ Did they have a firm handshake?
◆ What was their scent like?
◆ Is their beauty more than 'skin deep'?

Suspend, for a moment, your visual senses and see with your 'third eye'. Close your eyes, listen to someone's voice, pick up their scent, and maybe something indefinable about the set and shape of someone's body if they are walking close to you.

> I have two good friends, both of whom are totally blind. One has been blind from birth, and the other was blinded through an accident in his mid-forties. Both of them have an unerring ability to make accurate judgements, particularly with regard to relationships with people. I have told them that they can 'see more' about someone than a sighted person ever can. They both reacted in the same way when I said this. Their answer was, 'Of course we can – we use our third eye.'

I have discovered the value of this since I learned it from my friends. They pick up the vibes from people because all their other senses are so alert. Sighted people often use only one. For me, it's a combination of the sound of someone's voice, their touch as they shake your hand, or their sheer physicality – do they stand near to you, inappropriately close or far away?

Since using the 'third eye' approach, I have reduced the number of times I have made incorrect judgements about people. Believe me, over the years I've made a good few mistakes – some of them have been rather costly.

BUILDING RELATIONSHIPS WITH DIFFICULT PEOPLE

There's no doubt that at some time or other in your relationship-building process you will have to deal with some difficult people.

One of the best pieces of advice I ever received was from a highly successful financial director. I asked him if there was one particular thing to which he attributed his success. He said he had developed the combined skills of an acrobat, a diplomat and a doormat. The key to the issue, he thought, was knowing in which order and in what proportion these skills should be used!

Assertiveness

If you find it difficult working with high maintenance people or downright bullies, perhaps you should review your assertiveness techniques.

The key to being assertive is that, in any difficult situation, you leave that situation feeling okay about yourself and the other person involved. The aim is for a win–win outcome in terms of mutual respect and self-respect. Also there will be an absence of anxiety afterwards. You won't have feelings of guilt, embarrassment or frustration.

The difference between being aggressive, passive and assertive is clarified this way:

- An aggressive response is a put down. It is a personal attack, tinged with sarcasm and arrogance.

- A passive response is your choice not to say or do anything confrontational, but it can leave you feeling frustrated afterwards.

- An assertive response is a reasonable objection which is delivered in a polite and positive manner.

How do you normally respond to difficult situations? If you are going to get the most out of your personal contacts you will need to be able to think on your feet. If you find yourself in a tricky situation, an assertive response is one likely to be a win–win. You get nothing out of passive behaviour and you can lose a good deal from behaving aggressively, but what you can gain from being assertive is that you feel good about yourself and the other person. Once you have worked out what the tangible benefits are, it will make you more assertive in future.

> **Your boss asks you to work over the weekend for the second time this month. You know about the importance of the deadline, but it's your son's third birthday and you promised him you'd be at home all day and help with his party.**

What if you told your boss you've done your fair share already, having given up your previous weekend? You mention that your family life is suffering as a result and it's time he asked someone else.

Or you could resign yourself to the fact that working on your son's birthday is inevitable and go home and explain the situation to your partner and child. Then you will probably spend the whole of the weekend feeling both resentful and guilty.

You could say you have other commitments but suggest coming in early on Monday and offer to stay late a couple of evenings that week if that would help.

> **You work for a company with an established 'long hours culture' and it's wearing you out. You decide to cut back to a four-day week and prepare workable solutions to present to your directors.**

Your suggestions are turned down so you plead with them, explaining that the way you work is making life impossible.

You threaten to resign if they won't compromise.

Or you could ask for a detailed explanation from them as to why they have rejected your proposal. Once you've seen this, you could rework your proposal to counter their objections.

> **In a meeting, a colleague presents one of your ideas as her own. How do you react?**

You say nothing because you're worried about causing an argument in front of everyone, but you decide to have a word with her afterwards to set the record straight.

You express disbelief and firmly point out that this was your idea in the first place. You say you resent the fact that she's been underhand.

Why don't you say how pleased you are that she's backing you up? You could then invite her to work with you on the project.

> **You have an urgent project to complete, so you ask your assistant to help you. He says he has an even more important assignment to complete for another partner so he can't help.**

You try to bribe him to fit your work in, but realise that you'll probably have to do it yourself.

Try pulling rank and say there's no way this deadline can be missed. He has got to stay late and do the work.

Explain about the urgency, that the work has to be finished today. Offer to negotiate on his behalf about the other work he will have to lay aside to help you.

Overcoming difficulties

Sometimes when faced with a difficult situation, it seems easier to postpone dealing with the issue. Why is this so common? There are usually three reasons:

- Fear of being ignored.
- Fear of humiliation.
- Fear of being rejected.

Here are some suggestions to keep in mind when dealing with situations that require tact and diplomacy.

First, **acknowledge that there is a problem**. If you check your emotions, body sensations and thoughts, you will be in control of yourself. That will assist you in taking control of the issue.

Communicate carefully, clearly and positively. If appropriate (and possible) get support from a colleague or a superior.

Be flexible in your approach and review your goals – what outcome would be best, what are you realistically likely to achieve?

Don't procrastinate – act now to confront the challenge. A problem doesn't get any easier to deal with if it is ignored.

When engaging the other party, **pay attention** and listen without interrupting. Show that you understand how they feel as well as what they are saying.

Analyse the problem. It is crucial to differentiate between the facts (these sales figures are incorrect), assumptions (the calculations must have been prepared by junior members of staff), generalities (you never check your facts are right) and emotions (how can I possibly trust you?).

Respond quickly. If there is any action you can take immediately to make things better, do so. Focus on this rather than the cause of past grievances.

It is not necessary to take things personally. Do not give a flat 'No' answer and don't apportion blame. It is unwise to make promises you cannot keep. If possible retain a sense of humour – laughter can lower the temperature considerably.

Never view a client as a lost cause

If you think you are about to lose a client, do everything in your power to repair any damage done to the relationship. Great client recovery often leads to stronger and deeper relationships.

If you think you have lost the trust of a client, lose no time in trying to win back their confidence.

Some years ago I went through a complete rebranding exercise for the company I was running. Everything was re-vamped, including the personnel! One particularly conservative client felt she was being betrayed because I hadn't talked through my plans with her beforehand. She hated change.

For two weeks I could not get through to her on the phone. So I wrote to her explaining that despite the changes, I was still in control and nothing about our working relationship had altered.

Following a number of phone calls, she finally agreed to a meeting. The first half was unpleasant, while my client let rip with a tirade about my having let her down by not informing her of the changes in my company and I reassured her that it would not affect our relationship.

I listened to her concerns, and accepted responsibility for the way she had been treated. It took another couple of months before she would agree to try me out on another project. In effect, my re-branding had cost almost a year in convincing her that she could still trust me.

The lesson learned was that in future I always tried to take preventative measures to avoid a similar situation. Had I warned my client in advance of my business plans, this issue would not have occurred. Clients will feel reassured that their pain was more justified if they have a positive impact on your business.

Anger management

Is this going to be a confrontational exchange? I hope not!

♦ Do you ever get involved in conflict?

♦ Does your voice sometimes develop a hard edge?

♦ Have you ever slammed the phone down on someone?

♦ Do you behave towards others in an adult fashion?

♦ Does your inner child sometimes escape?

I am sure you've encountered someone at work or in a business relationship who has a tendency to 'throw their rattle out of the pram'. If you can adopt the techniques of a smooth operator, you will glide over a rock-strewn path with ease. It's all about confidence and chemistry.

You can help or hinder the situation by controlling your voice too. Your voice should contain no hint of annoyance, arrogance or nastiness, only obvious concern and interest for the other party. It transforms a battleground into a playground.

When someone is angry with you, move towards them verbally. If you are not on the defensive, it will stop them being so aggressive. If they are raising their voice, lower yours. Use open questions when enquiring about the problem. Look for ways to resolve the issue by suggesting some possible solutions. If in difficulty, 'suspend reaction'. If you don't ridicule, put down or resort to sarcasm, they can't keep fanning the flames.

When it is your turn to respond, stay calm. One angry person is quite enough. Be sympathetic. Show them that you understand and are anxious to deal with the problem. Tell them what you are prepared to do about it.

Allow people to express their anger. This way you will diffuse the situation. Keep your voice low pitched, stay in control and take notes. If the situation requires it, take responsibility for sorting out the problem.

Smoothing out problems

If you find you have some unexpected and unpleasant surprises to deal with, there are a few tips which could help. Whatever the situation, stay calm and smile if you can. Your mood will affect everyone around you. If you remain relaxed they are much more likely to help you sort out the problem.

Pause before you react. Don't turn a crisis into a catastrophe. There's no need for panic. An urgent problem can often be solved quite quickly. But first of all, get to the bottom of it. Find out exactly what is happening. You may not have had the full story from the person who first tells you about it.

Use your head! Have you ever been in a similar situation before? How did you handle it? If you have coped before, you can almost certainly do so again. The same solution may work this time, or you may have to get creative.

If the situation is going to need time to deal with, cancel meetings so that you have some spare capacity. Don't add to your problems by failing to turn up somewhere you are expected. If there are other people involved who could make the situation even more difficult, deal with them quickly but firmly.

Relish the unexpected. Rise to the challenge of dealing with a problematic situation. See it as an exciting aspect of your role as 'smooth operator'. If you are completely stuck, think about someone you admire or respect. Ask their advice – what would they do in the circumstances?

Dealing with criticism

When you are being 'got at' by someone, it is best to keep your cool. If you can listen without showing any negative or defensive emotions, you will make things easier for yourself.

As with listening skills, summarise the key points.

♦ Outline what the other person has said to make sure you've understood correctly.

♦ The more specific the criticism is, the more helpful it is.

♦ Find out, by asking questions, exactly what action has given rise to this particular situation.

♦ Was it the behaviour of one person?

- What impression have they formed and why was it unfavourable?

KEY POINT

Criticism is rarely groundless, but due to heightened emotions, can often be exaggerated. If you can extract the elements that are useful, they can be turned to positive advantage by acting differently in future to avoid a recurrence of the situation.

What other person makes them think like this? Try to see things from their perspective. Are they trying to help? Is it because they are under pressure themselves that they have behaved in this way.

You can always try a bit of flattery. Ask those responsible for raising the criticism for their help. By asking their advice and making them part of the solution strategy, they are likely to form a favourable impression of you. They could turn out to be influential as a mentor, coach or referrer, if handled correctly.

Always think positively. The people who criticise you have not only given you free information but have enabled you to improve your business strategy, planning or product. By implementing a solution you have taken positive steps to improve the future relationship.

Wherever possible, give praise. Whether it is the staff members who have helped you sort out the problem, or those who have raised the criticism in the first place, by praising others for what they have done well or contributed, you will reinforce the message that your behaviour is exemplary under difficult circumstances.

RESPECT AND TRUST

The establishment of trust and respect in a business relationship is paramount. Our ability to keep promises is what speaks volumes. Whether it's about keeping to time, returning calls, providing promised information, working to agreed budgets, whatever the issues, you need to be consistent.

It is when trust wavers that business contacts become shaky. If they cannot rely on your word, you will not be able to rely on them. You cannot make claims about your professional ability if you don't believe them and deliver them. No wonder business development is such a struggle and building brilliant connections is complicated. Nothing worth doing is achieved that quickly.

Another point to mention is that if you convince people about your trustworthiness, you need to reassure them that your motives are not self-centred. Self-preoccupation can wreck many good working relationships.

Also do not put yourself ahead of your contact's needs.

Arrogance, ego and the need to prove yourself right will work against the situation. Convince your contact that it is for his benefit that you are pursuing the relationship. When they believe this, you will gain from the relationship. Remember to be a 'giver' not a 'taker'.

Be transparent – make your objectives clear and understandable. In the chapter on communication, the importance of clarity over ambiguity is stressed. If your intentions are not made clear your contact will not know how best to help you.

Office politics

This can be a fairly fraught and troublesome area. It is said that there are only three types of people in business:

- The competent – they rise on merit.

- The incompetent – they rise because of a shortage of competent people.

- The political – they rise by taking credit from the competent while blaming the incompetent.

Take the time to find out who is who in your office hierarchy. You can work out where you stand, and where your colleagues and close team mates are 'in the food chain'.

- How does your boss fit in?

- Who is his manager?

- Do they both get along?

- Can you do anything to help your boss impress his seniors?

You don't necessarily have to be in a position of influence to provide powerful help. Simply handing in the report your manager asked for a couple of days early may make his life a lot easier. He could show it to his boss ahead of schedule which would put him in a good light.

Sharing information with him that possibly seems to you irrelevant or inconsequential could have far reaching effects, so don't shy away from listening to chatter at the coffee machine! You never know what you will hear or who you will meet.

DEVELOPING POWERFUL RELATIONSHIPS CHECKLIST

- Be transparent in your actions.

- Communicate with all sides as well as upwards and downwards.

- Network extensively to remain well informed.

- Identify and watch the 'politicians'.

- Put yourself in other people's shoes.

- Anticipate and manage others' reactions.

- Be clearly good at your job.

9

Relationships, Referrals, Results, Rewards

We must all learn the same way to get round corners.

Stephen Dando-Collins

This chapter starts with some R words.

◆ **Reaping rewards** through **referrals** for your company, your staff and for yourself.

◆ In all aspects of business **relationships**, know how to get a **response** to your efforts.

◆ Remember to switch to **receive** mode – no more transmitting. In this way favours can be **returned**.

◆ You'll feel enriched from new business, and **rewarding** contacts.

◆ It's a **reciprocal** exercise – what goes around, comes around.

- **Referrals** and **recommendations** will come to you regularly.

- **Repeat business** will be the norm.

Because you have worked at your networking, making connections and building relationships, your strategy is in place. There are, however, a few rules which should keep your relationship-building on track.

KEEP UP THE NUMBERS

If you find your new contacts decreasing, you could be stuck in a routine. If you do what you've always done, you'll get what you've always got. People make decisions about where they spend their time based on perceived worth. If the networking events you've been attending have lost their value to you, take a step back and have a look at your options for change.

Maybe you could vary the organisations you belong to, or the ways in which you seek to make new contacts.

Make a 'hit list' of new people you want to meet and try to contact between three and five each week. Build in a culture of asking your new contacts to introduce you to one or two new people and doing the same for them. This way your 'new blood' simply has to increase.

Speak to those people you have not contacted for over a year. Follow up those who have left organisations and moved on to pastures new. Build relationships with their successors and track down your old contacts. They will be flattered you have traced them and be happy to re-establish a connection with you. Who knows, they may just have been waiting for you to contact them.

Ask friends and colleagues to invite you to visit their business networking events as a guest.

It's sometimes a good idea to meet a completely new crowd. And what a great morale booster if you get there and someone recognises you.

THE FIVE RULES OF RELATIONSHIP-BUILDING

When breaking new ground, remember the five rules of relationship building.

Empathy

The ability to put yourself in the other person's position and see things from their point of view. It may come naturally to you, or you may have to acquire this skill. Empathy is vital and it has to be visible. Your business contact should feel that you understand. When you hear him say, 'You're a good person to work with' you can be assured you've got empathy!

To start the process, introduce yourself briefly and set about the task of finding some common ground as quickly as possible. It should be possible to establish two or three things in common with a new acquaintance within a minute or two.

Small talk should be used as a tool. The purpose is to uncover something that you have in common which will help establish rapport. Once you are no longer strangers, you have begun the process of establishing an individual connection. It is much easier to build a relationship once that stage has been reached.

Courtesy

Engage with someone by being sympathetic. It will surprise them and make them feel human. Small talk can so often seem superficial and artificial. Get into real conversation with your business contact and watch for the warmth of their reaction. Look for visual and verbal clues to assist in establishing the relationship. Make your voice warm and engaging and use positive body language. Watch for any signs of mirroring to help you.

Enquiry

Use open questions to elicit information and encourage conversation. If you're having difficulty in eliciting information from someone, it can be very frustrating being faced with just 'Yes' and 'No' answers. There is one technique which is called 'the string of pearls'. It means connecting one thought to another. You can try practising this technique during the small talk process at business events. Openers, such as a book you've just

read or a film you've recently seen, can be sufficient to
get you started.

Interest

Keep an expression of interest in what you are saying. Be
alert to the possibility of throwing in an unusual question
or witty response. Sometimes humour is appropriate to
maintain levels of attention. You can ask their opinion
about something as a hook for making a comment.
Don't forget to see the other person as someone of
importance – put yourself in their shoes. If you can use
this skill, you will 'humanise' your contact – after all,
that's how you'd like them to be thinking of you.

Respect

Never assume that your business contact will have the
same views and attitudes that you have. The world is
full of different people, all with differing ideas,
prejudices and opinions, and these may not be similar
to your own. Their culture may be very far removed
from yours, but that does not mean it is less important.
You may find some attitudes and customs unusual.
Working practices may seem positively odd. In order to
build a working relationship it is helpful to be able to
get on with business contacts. Argument and
confrontation is not the best basis for building rapport!

If you can understand your contact's attitudes and
customs, you may be able to respect these even if they
are wildly different to your own. Respect your contact's

individuality, and take account of what type of person you are dealing with. If you make a concerted effort to 'get on their wavelength' you will find this has a positive effect in subsequent dealings with them.

Be considerate of anything and everything that will indicate a caring manner, one that respects your contact's taste, views and attitudes. Your business contact will appreciate the attitude and respect this shows.

Make it real

I think sincerity is one of the most influential factors in relationship-building. No one is going to be interested in you if you're artificial. Be genuine. Know what you're talking about and mean what you say. If you're ignorant about the facts, whether it's to do with company policy, a particular area of expertise or specialist knowledge, you need to get out of the office and meet people who know the answers. Ask lots of questions and then listen.

Speak plainly. Don't use jargon and acronyms. It excludes people whether they are members of the general public or newcomers to your network or organisation. The more you can avoid these expressions creeping into your conversation, the better response you will receive from your business contact.

Give people a reason why they should respond to you. This should be some kind of benefit. If your business contact knows that you are able to organise deliveries at an earlier time in the morning, or collections later in the afternoon, they will be interested. Don't make promises if you can't deliver. Consider who you are dealing with – is he a donor, a user, a volunteer, a service provider? Depending on his role, his 'take' on the issue will be slightly different. Adjust your approach to reflect his interests.

If you are well informed and have all the key information to hand, this is all you'll need. Supposing you are trying to win over an influential new contact and he is passionate about golf. He has recently moved into the area and wants to know about the rules at the local club. You reckon that you'll earn yourself considerable goodwill if you assist him. Make sure the information you give him is correct and current. He won't be impressed if you assure him that obtaining membership is easy if there is actually a three-year waiting list to join!

People make decisions about others on the basis of both the rational and the emotional. Relationships are founded on certain values. Identify those values and make sure they are reciprocated. If they underpin everything you do, they will engage someone emotionally as well as intellectually.

Maintain brand identity where business relationships are concerned. You may not have the most expensive and impressive corporate house style or logo. But if you are neat and cohesive in your approach you will command interest and hopefully respect. Scrappy and unprofessional literature reflects poorly on your organisation and the service it offers.

> **KEY POINT**
>
> By maintaining high standards, personally and organisationally, your business contacts will recognise and respect your company's identity.

Your reputation directly affects the likelihood of developing a successful corporate relationship. If you are going to build strong business relationships you are clearly motivated by a deep sense of value. You are proud of who you are and what you do. Delivering outstanding service is not done just to win business.

You are developing relationships with other professionals who have the same sense of values. These are:

- honesty
- sincerity
- responsiveness
- confidence
- modesty
- trustworthiness
- appreciativeness.

REFERRALS ARE WONDERFUL

Word of mouth is a powerful tool – it is using other people as ambassadors for you, or your company.

If you offer to recommend your contacts and help them with their business development, they will reciprocate. It is possible to build a business entirely on referrals with the right network in place.

New business obtained on the recommendation of other people is highly profitable. The clients usually spend more and are loyal. But few companies actively seek referrals.

Pareto's law

The nineteenth century Italian mathematician, Pareto, gave his name to *Pareto's Law*. It is often known as the 80/20 rule.

It suggests that 80% of your business comes from about 20% of your clients.

A recent survey showed that almost 80% of a company's customers would be willing to act as referrers for them, but only 20% of them were asked to do so. A company that asks for referrals from 80% of its existing clients would increase its annual turnover by 20%.

Take time to organise and categorise your business contacts. Use this arrangement to help work out how you deal with them and how often you contact them.

Why referrals work

Referrals work because they come from a trusted source that has already benefited from the commercial or professional relationship yet has no vested interest in the business. It is independent and unsolicited. In business terms it has a rapid conversion rate – acceptance being dramatically accelerated because the service or product has already been tried and tested by a reputable third party.

When building brilliant business connections you are setting up the perfect mechanism for profiting by referrals. The key principles are 'giving to receive'.

Satisfied customers are both loyal and profitable. If you are always on the lookout for opportunities to recommend products or services which you trust and admire, you can expect this to work in your favour.

Make it a rule when beginning a business relationship to ask how you can help them.

What organisations or people do you know who could benefit from their services? If you build a 'rapport web' it can be an ever-increasing source of new business. Consider your business network's own contacts database, and so on. It's like ripples on a pond – self-perpetuating if you are persistent.

Don't be afraid to be direct. Make sure anyone who can offer a referral knows as much as possible about you or your company's services. If they do not understand the value of your product or services, or appreciate the key benefits, they will not realise what makes you outstanding and memorable. This is the message that they should be communicating.

Referrals are the rewards that come once you have created your network, made your connections and built your relationships. They are the ripe fruit that you have worked hard to grow. Like a harvest, they only appear if the conditions are favourable (i.e. if they are deserved).

Asking for referrals is one of the most powerful and low-cost ways of building or developing your career or business. It is a simple approach which feeds on its own success. But it has to be built on secure foundations.

When to ask for referrals
The time to ask for a referral is when:

- you've introduced someone to one of your contacts who awards them a project

- you have successfully completed at least two transactions for a client

- you solve a problem for someone who wants to reciprocate in some way

- someone thanks you for providing a good service

- you've helped someone through a particular difficulty.

If you are leaving referrals to chance and think of them only as an occasional welcome surprise, you are ignoring an essential part of your business development plan. Someone who knows you and your company are genuine and is prepared to pass on that information to an interested third party is worth his weight in gold.

When you were taking those first tentative steps outside your comfort zone, meeting new people, how did you feel? Nervous? Ill at ease? What about the occasion when your contact said, 'Oh, you must know my friend X?' Hearing a name that is familiar encourages you to respond positively in a given situation. I expect you visibly relaxed and began to build your brilliant business connection from that moment. That is exactly how a referral works. It's all about relationships, trust and respect.

Business success is built on the quality of the relationships we have with others. Relationships come in various and subtle shapes and sizes. Never assume you know what role a person has in an organisation. Inquire, investigate and direct your attentions appropriately. Collaborative relationships are the ones that you're attempting to build so you need to be knowledgeable as to how this is going to happen.

EVERY RELATIONSHIP IS DIFFERENT

Without business contacts, preferably positive ones, you will make little progress.

All your contacts are unique, some are demanding, others quite difficult, and some require understanding. Understanding them doesn't just make your relationship-building easier, it is inherent to the whole process. Where there is no understanding, how can a business relationship develop?

You must make sure you know enough about your business contacts to enable you to do a good job of rapport-building when you are with them. If not, you simply will not be taken seriously and you will lose credibility. Make sure you have background knowledge, and that it is noted somewhere. Add other information as you glean it – this could relate to your contact's current circumstances (a forthcoming marriage or an anticipated promotion).

KEY POINT

Accurate background information coupled with an empathetic approach will give you a winning formula.

Remember that your success in building brilliant business connections relates directly to your understanding of the other person – so make it your business to know as much about them as possible. That makes it much easier to build great rapport.

10

How Persuasive Are You?

I'll not listen to reason … Reason always means
what someone else has got to say.
*Elizabeth Gaskell (*Cranford*)*

ADVANCED RELATIONSHIP-BUILDING SKILLS

Whatever else needs to be done, however you try to
exert influence over the relationship-building process,
you need to be persuasive in your dealings with your
potential clients, influencers and recommenders. By
whatever means you attempt to put across your case,
you should try to set yourself apart from your
competitors or other contenders in the relationship-
building process. It is only by being memorable and
outstanding that you will be preferred.

You should bear in mind that other people are
attempting to reach a similar position to yours. If you
have researched and found that a particular person is an
ideal business contact, it is safe to assume that others
will have done the same. Assume that they are as
professional as you are.

Building successful business relationships is a complex process. Contacts want to decide 'their' way whether or not to do business with

you. They want to think about the proposition you are making to them, to assess it and make what they would regard as a considered decision. Their thinking, as we have mentioned, is made up from many differing viewpoints. If you imagine there are two identical cases on a set of scales, how do you end up on the winning side?

To be an effective persuader you should be able to communicate the following points to your contact:

+ he is important and will be treated as such
+ his opinions and position are respected
+ he will be dealt with as a unique individual
+ there are benefits available to him in dealing with you
+ what the facts are
+ any snags there are (and there usually are some)
+ what compromises will be required
+ how the relationship can work.

WHAT DEFINES 'PERSUASIVE'?

As an effective persuader your approach needs to be seen by your chosen business contact as:

+ understandable
+ attractive

♦ convincing.

None of these on their own is enough to secure a brilliant business relationship. They need to be strong enough jointly to set you ahead of any other parties trying to negotiate arrangements with your contact.

To be convincing and effective, your approach to rapport-building must be individually tailored to the other party involved in the process. If your usual ploy is to offer your business contact corporate hospitality to a sporting event, this is not going to cut much ice with someone who is mad about opera or the arts. Each business contact wants an approach which they see respects their point of view, matches their personality and interests and so generates more immediate response and interest.

Bearing this in mind will get you off along the right track. It should quickly show you the reason why the identification and preparation stages are so important. This is complex and there are many things to consider, including your own personal positioning.

If handled smoothly, the relationship-building process will appear well thought out and relevant – because that's exactly what it is! Your contact will know that he is dealing with a professional who takes time and care over each contact he makes and treats each one with respect.

Make what you say attractive

Communicate clearly, make your words attractive so that your business contact wants to listen and is as keen to develop the relationship as you are. How do you do this?

Talk about the benefits. People do not encourage relationships in business just for friendship. It has to go further than that. They will want a clearly-defined purpose. If you explain the reasons why you want to connect with them and that there are advantages to you both, they will understand 'what's in it for them'.

The advantages, say, of a small specialist design group collaborating with a large architectural practice means that the small firm can be included in bigger projects than they would normally get involved in. The large company will harness external specialist expertise in an area they do not have covered in-house. Working together to bid for significant projects will result in a win–win solution.

Talking benefits in this way as you describe your ideas for increased working opportunities will support the relationship-building process. It is important to get this right. All contacts are different and in some cases you will be persuading more than one person of the advantages of such an alliance. For example, you could be required to influence a board of directors, or a group of partners in a professional service firm.

COMMUNICATE WITH EVERYONE

Communicate with everyone, respect their opinion, value their contribution, gain from the experience. In defining persuasion, it is important to make what you say to your business contact credible.

Most people who are experienced in business dealings have a healthy degree of scepticism. They can be forgiven for thinking that you have a vested interest and will be looking for an element of 'proof'.

The main form of evidence has to be the persuasiveness of the case put forward, harnessed to the tangible business benefits, followed by proof positive that it can be done. By reporting that 'Two years ago we collaborated with Company X who were looking to expand in Europe. Because of our strong associations in France, Germany and Spain, we were able to open up new markets for them in these countries.' This will show your new potential partner that you have a proven track record that backs up the proposal.

Such compelling evidence would help to convince even the most cynical business contact. There is factual, physical proof here. Your contact can go and check the record and be reassured that what you say is true and not a fabricated claim.

If you find that your claim needs further substantiation, it may be helpful if there are outside elements that can be utilised. Perhaps your professional association has written a report about the achievements made by you and your previous partner firm. There may be other independent parties who are aware of your successful alliance. Maybe you made a presentation to another organisation, or wrote a paper for a professional journal.

There are a number of ways external proof can be harnessed. These independent authorities are powerful persuasive elements in building credibility with your proposed partner. You can probably think of other examples applied to your own company or area of expertise. Whatever your profession, industry or sector, by assembling all possible independent proof factors you can use them appropriately when required.

ADD VALUE

You may be able to strengthen your power to persuade if you have elements of added value that you can bring to the relationship-building process. This will depend very much on your individual expertise or company policy. However, if you can offer:

- more than usual
- more than the competition
- more than expected

this could have irresistible appeal to your business contact.

You could, for instance, suggest that you have a trial period of three months of the service, an incentive, an aspect of the collaboration that you can offer 'pro bono' – particularly in relation to a charity or not-for-profit organisation.

Any such device as this can act in a number of different ways to:

- help you get a better hearing
- help improve the weight of the case you can present
- persuade people to act now rather than later.

However you choose to persuade people of the benefits of your mutual business relationship, this can only be part of your organised rapport-building strategy. Some suggestions will work better than others. You may be able to control parts, but you will not be able to control all of the process.

HUMOUR

Use humour to improve creativity and lower stress. In your dealings with other people, the ability to use humour can work wonders. It aids communication, establishes empathy, diffuses awkward situations, and even builds the bottom line.

Studies show that humour can increase productivity because it:

- increases the immune system's activity
- decreases stress hormones which constrict blood vessels
- increases the antibody immunoglobulin A.

If you use or experience positive humour it involves the whole brain, not just one side. The result is better coordination between both sides. This means you are more relaxed, your blood pressure and heart rate are lowered and you are able to think more clearly.

If those are the benefits to you, imagine how persuasive you will sound to your business contact.

TIP

It is important to stress here that it is positive, not negative humour, that works wonders. Sarcasm, irony, insults and black humour are not helpful. Avoid all forms of sexist, racist, crude and mean-spirited remarks. They work in reverse.

When you are trying to woo your new business contact, there are plenty of opportunities to show an appropriate sense of humour during a meeting. For instance, when awkward pauses arise, papers are misplaced or unexpected interruptions occur, it is far cooler to just 'go with the flow'.

Being flexible shows an ability to be relaxed. You can often get an impression of whether humour is appreciated by looking around you. If you are in someone's office, for instance, are there any amusing signs, cartoons, slogans or pictures? Do other people seem relaxed and able to joke with each other?

KEY POINT

When people have to decide whether to work or collaborate with you or not, they will be influenced by how they feel about you. By including humour in your dealings with other people, you are encouraging them to like you.

Laughter reduces stress because it is relaxing and calming. It has been shown in hospitals that patients who have had 'humour therapy' recover quicker from illnesses or surgery than those who do not laugh.

If you are trying to build rapport within your organisation, the first time a new employee laughs at an 'inside joke' shows that he's part of a team with his co-workers. You know you have an 'inside joke' when everybody from a group laughs but no one outside the group does.

How many times have you noticed that when you are stressed you fumble, drop things or make mistakes? It is a myth that laughter is trivial. On the contrary – it is very powerful. Even just smiling can be healing and reassuring.

On one occasion I was attending an important job interview. I was desperate to be successful because it was a position I really wanted. The interviewer was a rather serious man who remarked, when looking at my CV, that my first job had been in the House of Lords. 'Yes, that's right,' I responded, 'and I've been working my way steadily downwards ever since.'

'In that case you won't fit in here,' was his swift reply. He had not appreciated the joke. Needless to say, I didn't get the job. I now exercise great caution when using self-deprecating remarks!

11

How Powerful Personal Connections Can Increase the Bottom Line

A wise man will make more opportunities than
he finds.

Francis Bacon

Harnessing the power of personal connections builds
strong and lasting relationships. You are looking for
ways to match people, organisations and opportunities.

Try to develop your own skills with regard to
relationship-building throughout your company's
network. The better thought out, innovative and sincere
relationships are likely to be more profitable. You
should put equal emphasis on your internal
relationships with colleagues, staff and superiors and the
external ones – existing and new customers, suppliers
and referrers.

What will help you do this? Here are a few T words to
consider.

- Establishing **trust** – respect your business contacts and your staff. They will respond in a positive way.

- Remember to say **thank you** – it costs you nothing and gains you much.

- If someone says '**thank goodness** we met', **treasure** that moment.

- You may get **testimonials** from satisfied clients or recommenders.

- When other people blow your **trumpet** for you the sound is much louder!

- You will find your **thinking** processes have changed. You will be far more people-oriented – whether externally or internally.

- With **tenacity** these relationships will flourish.

HOLD ON TO YOUR ASSETS

Before moving on to more advanced methods of dealing with external business contacts, let's look inside the company for a moment.

Many organisations know that staff hold the key to success but few realise how to capitalise on their greatest asset. So often companies focus on meeting customer needs or increasing the bottom line and forget that its employees can make it happen.

Good practice for people management is a variable process, but some of the main factors involved here are:

- enlightened leadership culture

- staff involvement at every level in the organisation

- staff development to make employees feel valued and challenged

- flexible work patterns to meet the needs of both the business and staff.

If you knew it was going to cost you three times as much to replace a member of staff than to retain one, what would you do? Not exactly a difficult question, I hope. But how many people really pay attention to this?

When a company loses a key member of staff they often are the last to realise that it would have been much cheaper to tackle the issues that made those people quit rather than go through the expensive steps needed to replace them.

The real impact on businesses that lose staff regularly and are constantly recruiting new ones is that it probably takes a year's salary to arrive at 'break-even' point. By that I mean the time reached when the new member of staff turns from being a net cost to adding value.

Consider the case of a senior manager who leaves after, say, two years' service. In replacing him, the company will pay a recruitment agency, allocate HR administrators and involve directors in interviews. The two years of training investment will have disappeared. There will be loss of productivity in the run-up to his departure. His staff will be demotivated and, until the replacement is up to speed, may lose momentum and direction.

Above all, and this is where the real cost lies, all his business relationships will disappear with him. When you consider the reasons why he resigned – if indeed you ever know them – would it not have been cheaper and easier to pay attention to those issues and retain the manager? Was it a salary factor? Was it his boss? Perhaps he felt undervalued.

Whatever the solution – and it may not have been simple – it would have been cheaper to address those than to replace a key member of staff. If you value your staff as assets, not just overheads, and retain them and their business relationships, you will save your company significant amounts of money.

Realise their potential

Let's leave the financial issues for a moment. The subject is valuing staff, maximising their potential and regarding them as tangible assets.

People can, and do, make an enormous difference to any organisation. What motivates and drives them to release their potential is the way they are treated by their company. So how do you go about building brilliant business connections amongst staff?

Firms need to find creative ways of motivating employees, sharing knowledge with them for the benefit of the whole organisation. It could be an environmental issue – such as the provision of a pleasant café area for informal meetings, or the colour scheme and furnishings of the office area. It could be a change in the managerial and organisational culture.

What about a different dress code – something more informal if the company has a predominantly young staff? Flexible working patterns would be popular if a number of the staff have young children.

Bringing in emphasis on creativity through redesign of work areas or working conditions can make a huge impact on staff morale. Happy staff will remain with the company. If HR and recruitment costs drop, the increase in the company's bottom line is significant.

Giving recognition for good service
Developing a 'praise culture' is something some enlightened firms practise. This can be applied in a number of ways – such as public praise for good work, support for entry to industry award competitions and

more social opportunities.

Positive moves including new training methods, cutting-edge technology and introducing a profit-sharing scheme for individual staff on the basis of performance could be other winning formulae for improved staff retention.

Organisations that practise good people management find it brings many benefits including financial success and retention of key staff and their business connections.

EXTERNAL RELATIONSHIPS

Applying the same principle in another way, it costs a quarter of the amount to retain an existing client than it does to win a new one. If you can keep your clients happy, you will make business development easier and more successful.

One of the most effective ways of harnessing the power of personal connections in an external way is to use it to develop your business. You can extend the relationship-building process for the specific purpose of increasing turnover by simply enquiring and listening.

A customer satisfaction survey

In essence, I am talking about a customer satisfaction survey. Why is it important to find out customer feedback? Because it is an essential piece of management information. For professional service firms, customer feedback can be a remarkably inexpensive source of market research.

You can find out:

- who your customers are
- if they are likely to be your customers
- why they are your customers and not someone else's
- what your customers want
- how your customers feel
- what your customers think
- how you can make your customers feel valued
- what sort of initiatives your customers would appreciate
- what you can do to keep your customers loyal
- how you can give yourself a competitive edge over others.

There is a huge amount of information here and it should be available for use by the management structure to increase turnover and improve the bottom line. Many successful companies use this method to enhance corporate connections and reinforce existing business relationships. You may not need to answer all these questions but you should take the trouble to find out as much as you can about the psychology of your customers. If you don't know what's happening, you won't know how to deal with situations when they occur.

If you take the time to talk to people who already do business with you, who have paid money for your services, you will be asking their advice, and that is flattering. In turn they will feel that their opinions matter. They are less likely to desert you in times of difficulty if you have made them feel important.

Monitoring customer satisfaction is a pointless activity unless management have a sense of ownership for the process and are prepared to act on the results.

> **One company succeeded in increasing their annual turnover by up to one fifth by managing a tailored approach.**

The objective of the survey has to be defined before the programme begins, together with a budget and a timetable.

Before embarking on such a survey, it is useful to review existing information or research data concerning customers and customer satisfaction. You could ask:

- what you know about your existing customers
- what you know about their expectations
- how well you are meeting those expectations
- what will happen to customer requirements in the future
- how you compare to your competitors

◆ how the market is likely to change in the next three
years.

Case study
Following a rebranding exercise three years ago,
Company X decided to carry out some empirical
research to assess how the new brand values and
perceptions of the business generally had changed
and/or improved. This was conducted by means of a
survey of their clients, potential clients, and market
influencers.

The research was designed to give a clear indication
of the competitive market position that X currently
occupied and to point to the effectiveness of the
firm's different services and market sectors. It was
also to show how they fitted with the image, identity
and reputation that it projected overall.

In addition it highlighted the relative strengths and
weaknesses as observed by a representative cross-
section, whose opinions were specific and insightful.
It offered opportunities for the future as well as areas
where increased marketing activities would produce a
measurably greater return on investment.

The most important result of the survey was the
influence it brought to the firm's strategy for building
further value into their brand for the future. It helped
clarify issues surrounding the way to create best
market differentiation so that it could compete even
more successfully with its known competitors.

The research asked the following questions of the three categories of influences.

Existing clients

- Reasons and motivations for choosing X in the first place.

- Satisfaction levels in the relationship.

- Satisfaction with final results.

- How X's character is perceived: innovative, conservative, in tune with needs, prestigious, dependable, friendly, formal, etc.

- Relative strengths compared to others in the marketplace.

- Relative weaknesses compared to others in the marketplace.

- Extent to which they (the client) would refer business and for what specific product/service/application.

- Awareness and effect of the new branding.

- Relative strengths of different market-facing divisions.

Prospective clients

- Familiarity with, and knowledge about, X together with perceptions of its relative market positioning.

- Values associated with the brand (plus any historical perceptions).

- What factors most influence choice – referral, reputation, track record, the quality of individuals, relevance of previous projects.

- Who's who in the marketplace and their relative strengths and weaknesses.

- Expectations of service performance.

- Expectations of individuals.

- Extent to which X could/would be referred to others.

Market influencers/referrers
- Extent and nature of reputation.
- Effect of the rebranding.
- Quality of the people.
- Quality of service/results.
- Specific areas where X would be referred.
- Specific areas where it probably would not.
- Relevance/value of different product areas.
- Suggestions for product/service development.

Method
The directors of X decided the specific areas and outcomes required from the research survey questions. They developed a questionnaire for each of the three categories above and included a mix of closed and open-ended questions to capture opinions and perceptions.

From their database they selected and approached a

similar number of companies from each of the three categories. There was a need to modify the questions after one or two phone calls had not produced the desired results.

After completing the survey, they analysed the results. The report showed the analysis, drew conclusions and made recommendations from what the contacts and clients had said.

Conclusions

The overall results were positive and showed a universally high regard for X's professionalism and confidence in its ability to deliver consistently well-above-average results. The principals were considered to be approachable and well able to handle any difficulties in the relationships between X and their clients.

It indicated that X was successful in its relationship-building events – it had a reputation for quality events even from people who had never attended one!

It was recognised that X had been increasing its marketing and PR presence to maintain a modern image while at the same time raising its profile.

In common with many professional service companies, X's directors were not only the principal practitioners of the work in terms of fee earners but were also required to manage the business. There was a consistently high regard for X's professional capability but there was room for improvement in terms of its business relationship-building.

It was evident from the research that contact databases would benefit from regular updating. There were inconsistencies in terms of a business development strategy and this would be beneficial if X were to effect a more integrated approach.

Successful outcomes
Six months later, X were delighted to announce that following the creation of the post of Business Development Director, the company had won a significant number of new projects. The results were tangible; by applying an integrated and consistent approach to business relationship building, X's annual turnover had increased by 19%.

If you take that one stage further, to increase a company's annual turnover by almost 20% by means of a customer satisfaction survey, a small- to medium-sized company with an annual turnover of £2m would add on an extra £400,000 in a year.

Significant? How can you afford to ignore it? It's most likely there, waiting for you, just for the asking!

WAYS TO FURTHER DEVELOP PROFESSIONAL RELATIONSHIPS

Partnering – strategic alliances

Are you constantly searching for ways to grow your business? Are you seeking new ideas that will positively impact on your clients' bottom lines (and yours)? Try exploring concepts that will highlight your brilliance.

Do not overlook your competition. Shifting your focus to view the competition as a resource rather than a rival allows you to discover opportunities that would otherwise remain unknown to you.

Thinking of competitors as allies rather than rivals is not really new. Strategic alliances are often the way forward for small- to medium-sized firms. Co-operation with competitors, customers, suppliers and companies producing complementary products can expand markets and lead to the formation of new business relationships and, in extreme cases, create new forms of enterprise.

> **KEY POINT**
>
> Co-operation makes more sense than competition. The idea of teaming up with competitors to develop new ideas and to make your company better at what is does delivers a challenge to many people.

Strategic alliances can be formal and encompass a specific project. At other times they are informative and active with only certain types of projects.

Development or extension of products or services
If your company is client-focused, you will actively seek
out the best ideas and ways of serving your clients'
needs.

Combining strengths can produce amazing results. By
collaborating with a competitor you might be able to
win new contracts that neither of you could do alone.
One plus one can often equal much more than two!

Apportioning referrals
Consider having at least three people or companies in
your database to whom you would refer business
without hesitation. There may be a mutual
understanding that the favour will be returned. Whether
you have arranged a referral fee, a reciprocal referral,
or you are the one that wins the project, everyone is a
winner.

It is essential to know the best firms producing the
complementary or related services in your own market.
Knowledge is power and if your clients perceive you as
the place to go for information, your business
reputation will grow. Your clients will value your
knowledge and connections in the market.

Knowledge of best practice
You can learn something from everyone and every
situation. No one can possibly have all the answers, and
that is why sharing best practice is so important.

Sharing best practices does not
mean sharing trade secrets or
colluding on fees. It means coming
together for improvement.

KEY POINT

True professionals subscribe to the
principle of abundance and see the
power of helping each other to get
better. 'A rising tide lifts all boats.'

Risk awareness

It is important to bear in mind the
possible pitfalls when contemplating strategic alliances
with a competitor, or anyone else.

One possible issue is the lack of common goals amongst
the parties. If the collaboration does not work, perhaps
the synergies were not real or the communication
system was flawed. It is wise to do some research before
committing yourself to such an alliance – a corporate
version of the prenuptial agreement!

The obvious benefits of strategic alliances mostly
outweigh the risks. It is important to pay attention to
whether you really can work together. Complementary
areas of expertise are one thing, but do the personality
types fit together? The question to ask is, 'Can they
really add value to the project?'

Creating successful strategic alliances is a valuable skill
to acquire. You need to have complete awareness of
your own strengths and weaknesses, as well as those of
your company. Look for complementary strengths in
your competitor-cum-ally. Ideally it will be someone
who actually makes you look better at what you do.

Always be open-minded to new opportunities and collaborations. You could seek out movers and shakers in your industry or profession. They would regard it as an innovative way to progress and it is another potentially valuable way of harnessing the power of brilliant business connections.

12

Summary – Checklists for Success

WHO NEEDS BUSINESS CONNECTIONS ANYWAY?

♦ Task-awareness is fine, but being passionate about people will take you further faster.

♦ Do people mean business? Yes!

The two main reasons why you should harness the power of personal connections are:

♦ Your company will be more successful. It will stand out ahead of its competitors.

♦ You will progress further and faster along your career path than someone who doesn't.

Personal recommendations speak volumes and are more impressive than the best CV.

Developing successful relationships at work means two things:

♦ internally (within the organisation or profession)

- externally (among clients, work providers, suppliers).

In both cases, it helps to be confident and have extrovert characteristics.

How do you distinguish between networking, connecting and relationship-building?

- As a means of generating business or career progression, a strategic networking plan is essential.

- From this, you should have the ability to establish unique personal and professional connections.

- These connections should be nurtured so that brilliant business relationships are developed.

- There are certain key attitudes and actions you can use to maximise success. It is not important what system you adopt as long as it works for you.

- Make sure the chosen system is appropriate to your needs and that it connects with your company's marketing and business development strategy.

The qualities needed to build good rapport with business connections:

- Belief in yourself.
- Belief in your company.
- Meeting lots of people.
- Listening to your new business contacts.
- Maintaining a sense of humour.
- Re-visiting existing contacts regularly.

- Offering and accepting referrals from everyone you meet.
- Following-up on every connection made.
- Ensuring that the relationship is reciprocal.

R FOR RELATIONSHIPS

- **Relationships** – Why build them? Two reasons: because it's practical and profitable. The most successful people are the best connected.

- **Recognition** – Creating impact when you meet people. Never underestimate the power of first impressions.

- **Recall** – If someone can recall you easily to mind, you've made (hopefully) a favourable effect when you first were introduced.

- **Reaction** – One of the things you are hoping for is a positive reaction when you encounter them again.

- **Respect** – Aim to gain their trust. The ability to co-operate with and assist others is vital. You will then earn respect. Don't forget to show it to others in return.

- **Responsibility** – You should take responsibility for your business relationships. That will keep you in control of your personal network. It's worth a lot to you – don't let others mess it up.

Everyone has their own group of personal contacts – their unique network. How many people are in yours? Do you value it? How do you use it?

Here are some ways in which it can be used:

- as a research aid, for information gathering
- as a link to new clients or markets
- to advance your career by seeking influential people.

KEY STAGES IN THE BRILLIANT BUSINESS RELATIONSHIPS PROCESS

Strategic networking requires the following action steps:

- Reviewing your existing contacts and connections.

- Updating these.

- Identifying who you need to get to know better.

- Seeing how much knowledge you have of these people and how much they know about you.

- Seeing what gaps there are in your company's network and how it is planned to fill these gaps.

- Looking at the policy/action plan regarding corporate events/entertaining.

- Considering a regular review meeting for business relationship development.

- Developing your rapport-building web/establishing targets and measuring results regularly.

- Checking if any recent 'customer satisfaction surveys' have been carried out.

- If they have, analysing the information they yielded and the use that was made of it.

HOW TO MAXIMISE SUCCESS AND CONTINUE DEVELOPMENT

Vary your approach to relationship-building. Here are five ways:

Business network connections

By designing and building a unique business network system you can track the effectiveness of contacts, collaborators, strategic alliances, complementary firms, products and services. They can add value in so many ways.

Connecting individuals

By harnessing the power of personal connections you can utilise to your best advantage networks, connections and relationships. Individuals can offer tailored introductions to you to help you with your career progression or business development.

Connecting with customers

If you use your individual connections wisely you can develop connection strategies to win, retain and develop new business. By means of regular audits of existing and past customer relationships you can win new projects and open up new markets.

Connecting with staff

Be passionate about relationship-building within your company and empowering individuals and teams. It is possible to deliver outstanding results by encouraging connections between employees and employers.

Discreet connections

If you have sensitive business connections – potential sales and acquisitions of a business division, investment procurement or executive searches and headhunting projects – by using your unique professional network, solutions are often found speedily and successfully.

PERSISTENCE PAYS

To harness the power of personal connections you need to keep a few 'P' words in mind.

- **Persistence** pays, there's no doubt about that.

- Relationship-building is like **planting seeds** – they take time to germinate.

- One of the most important factors in the process is **preparation**.

- You need to prepare the ground – it pays to know about your **prospects**.

- You have to **persevere** – sometimes for months and, in some cases, years.

- Try to be unfailingly **polite** and **patient**.

- A **positive** mental attitude and outlook is infectious.

- **Persuasion** tactics get easier with **practice**.

- Make sure you do some **planning** – it helps you to know when and how to keep in contact.

- Don't underestimate the value of **praise** when communicating with your business contacts.

- Most people respond **positively** to flattery.

SAY IT WITH FEELING

What's important is the way you begin to build business relationships. In effect you're starting a process of persuasion. It's not easy, and often using words is just not enough.

- You have to be able to hook the other party into the idea that there is something in it for them.

- To be persuasive you should offer people reasons that reflect their point of view.

- Benefits are things that do something for people.

- The benefits of reading this book include helping you with your strategy for building brilliant business connections!

Touching emotions and intellect

- To be an effective persuader you should not only offer good reasons for something but also create emotional goodwill at the same time.

- If you need to persuade powerfully, bring in stories to connect with people's hearts as well as minds.

REFERRALS WORK WONDERS

- If you have mutual connections, it is much easier to persuade others when there are credible people to testify that your skills helped them in some way or other.

Use several sources

♦ If possible, don't rely on one source for recommendations. Using several different parties gives further weight to your case.

♦ You increase your chances that one or other of your sources will be a powerful influence over the person with whom you're building up trust.

DON'T WASTE THEIR TIME

♦ Think about how you want to come across to your business contact.

♦ Ask yourself why anyone should want to listen to you.

♦ List your reasons and then organise them.

♦ What are the most important things you are trying to say?

♦ How can you build rapport with one another?

♦ Can you arrange your thoughts into a logical sequence? You could start with something attention-grabbing and continue to maintain interest throughout the exchange. Perhaps you want to build up your case throughout the dialogue and end with some weighty fact that has masses of impact.

CHECK PROGRESS

By using a simple achievement matrix you can check progress and remind yourself of your continual plan for refreshing and reviving your brilliant business connections.

Step 1

- Review your contacts database and list your achievements and successes over the last month.

- How many new contacts have you added?

- How many existing contacts did you manage to reach – and were these by telephone, email or face-to-face meetings?

Step 2

- List the obstacles that you have overcome and those that are currently to be solved.

- Was it a time-management issue?

- Did you attend a sufficient number of networking events?

- Did you develop the appropriate method of communication?

Step 3

- Make a note of the action you will need to take to resolve the latest obstacles.

- Do you need to phone more people?

- Have you progressed certain connections as far as possible?

- Are you awaiting information from other people which they promised you?

- Have you followed through with the information, introductions, etc., that you have offered people in your network?

Step 4
- List the objectives for the next period.

- How many people do you wish to connect with by the end of the month?

- What percentage of these are existing contacts and how many are new introductions?

- Are the work-getting targets progressing according to plan?

COMMUNICATION SKILLS AWARENESS CHECKLIST

- **Presence**. Pay attention to the way your voice and body language are used in conjunction with the words you speak. You can convey the right impression if they are used correctly.

- **Relating**. Don't underestimate the importance of developing your rapport-building skills to get on the same wavelength as your business prospect.

- **Questioning**. When engaged in conversation with your contact, make sure you match your question to the situation or subject. Beware of asking irrelevant questions – this will show that you've not paid attention to what he said.

- **Listening**. Listen to everything he says attentively. Try to reach at least Level Four. If he's likely to become a significant influence in your business development strategy you should aim to achieve Level Five eventually.

- **Checking**. The art of glancing at your business contact to see that he's still on your wavelength while you're engaged in dialogue. Watch for gestures and see whether he does the same when he's talking to you.

CHECKLIST FOR DEVELOPING POWERFUL RELATIONSHIPS

- Be transparent in your actions.

- Communicate with all sides as well as upwards and downwards.

- Network extensively to keep yourself well informed.

- Identify and watch the 'politicians'.

- Put yourself in other people's shoes.

- Anticipate and manage others' reactions.

- Be clearly good at your job.

Every relationship is different

- Without business contacts, preferably positive ones, you will make little progress.

- All your contacts are unique, some are demanding, others quite difficult, and some require understanding.

- Understanding them doesn't just make your relationship-building easier, it is inherent to the whole process.

- Where there is no understanding, how can a business relationship develop?

In essence the key to building brilliant business connections is being sincere:

- Establish **trust** – respect your business contacts and your staff. They will respond in a positive way.

- Remember to say **thank you** – it costs you nothing and gains you much.

- If someone says '**thank goodness** we met' – **treasure** that moment.

- You may get **testimonials** from satisfied clients or recommenders.

- When other people blow your **trumpet** for you the sound is much louder!

- You will find your **thinking** processes have changed. You will be far more people-oriented – whether externally or internally.

- With **tenacity**, relationships will flourish.

AND FINALLY...

If you harness the power of personal connections, you will realise the importance of five words:

- enquire
- listen
- offer
- trust
- respect.

My consultancy helps firms and individuals make connections that build strong and lasting relationships. Not only do I match people, organisations and opportunities: I coach, mentor and train on the importance of relationship-building through a business's own network. I can deliver better, innovative and more profitable relationships with existing and new customers, suppliers and employees.

I hope this book has helped you to recognise the power that relationship-building has to make business and people management easier and more effective.

Remember, it's people that matter, not skills, education, qualifications or experience. People do business with people they like and trust. When developing brilliant business connections, small talk really means big business!

Index

If you want to know how...

- ◆ To buy a home in the sun, and let it out
- ◆ To move overseas, and work well with the people who live there
- ◆ To get the job you want, in the career you like
- ◆ To plan a wedding, and make the Best Man's speech
- ◆ To build your own home, or manage a conversion
- ◆ To buy and sell houses, and make money from doing so
- ◆ To gain new skills and learning, at a later time in life
- ◆ To empower yourself, and improve your lifestyle
- ◆ To start your own business, and run it profitably
- ◆ To prepare for your retirement, and generate a pension
- ◆ To improve your English, or write a PhD
- ◆ To be a more effective manager, and a good communicator
- ◆ To write a book, and get it published

If you want to know how to do all these things and much, much more...

If you want to know how...to present with power

"Your ability to communicate is the single most important factor in your professional tool bag. People who make a difference, who inspire others, who get promoted, are usually excellent communicators. The people who have shaped the course of history were all excellent communicators. They could move audiences, win minds and hearts and get people to take action.

The need to communicate is even greater in today's fast-changing workplace. Of all the ways you communicate, the one that gives you the greatest chance to make a powerful impact is the presentation.

This book covers all you need to know about researching your material, structuring your message and designing your visual aids, it also shows you ways to develop confidence and gives tips on how to deliver. Whether you are a novice speaker or a seasoned pro, this book will give you tips and techniques that will take you to the next level."

Shay McConnon

Presenting with Power
Captivate, motivate, inspire and persuade
Shay McConnon

'Shay's raw talent together with his passion for the audience and his material make for a magical experience.' *Siemens*

"His engaging style of presentation captivates his audience whatever their background or current state of motivation."
Director, Walkers Snack Foods

ISBN 1 84528 022 9

If you want to know how...to resolve conflict in the workplace

Margaret and Shay McConnon show you how to manage disagreements and develop trust and understanding. They enable us to begin meeting our needs and those of the other person, while maintaining the relationship and resolving our differences respectfully.

Resolving Conflict
How to manage disagreements and develop trust and understanding
Shay and Margaret McConnon

"One of the best books I have read on conflict resolution in my 30+ years in the field." Mediation Office The World Bank

"...Readable and accessible." *The Times*

"...contains great ideas, simply explained, to be put into practice by those in the workplace who'd not only like to manage conflicts that typically occur but also prevent them." – Dr Pam Spurr, Psychologist and life coach, LBC Radio

ISBN 1 85703 944 0

How To Books are available through all good bookshops, or you can order direct from us through Grantham Book Services.

Tel: +44 (0)1476 541080
Fax: +44 (0)1476 541061
Email: orders@gbs.tbs-ltd.co.uk

Or via our website

www.howtobooks.co.uk

To order via any of these methods please quote the title(s) of the book(s) and your credit card number together with its expiry date.

For further information about our books and catalogue, please contact:

How To Books
3 Newtec Place
Magdalen Road
Oxford OX4 1RE

Visit our web site at
www.howtobooks.co.uk

Or you can contact us by email at info@howtobooks.co.uk